T0129427

Live Alive

*The Truth About Your Life and
How to Be Your Own Master*

ALINA HAIDUC SUKUMARAN

BALBOA.
PRESS

A DIVISION OF HAY HOUSE

Balboa Press books may be ordered through booksellers or by contacting:

Balboa Press
A Division of Hay House
1663 Liberty Drive
Bloomington, IN 47403
www.balboapress.com
1 (877) 407-4847

Because of the dynamic nature of the Internet, any web addresses or links contained in this book may have changed since publication and may no longer be valid. The views expressed in this work are solely those of the author and do not necessarily reflect the views of the publisher, and the publisher hereby disclaims any responsibility for them.

The author of this book does not dispense medical advice or prescribe the use of any technique as a form of treatment for physical, emotional, or medical problems without the advice of a physician, either directly or indirectly. The intent of the author is only to offer information of a general nature to help you in your quest for emotional and spiritual well-being. In the event you use any of the information in this book for yourself, which is your constitutional right, the author and the publisher assume no responsibility for your actions.

Any people depicted in stock imagery provided by Getty Images are models, and such images are being used for illustrative purposes only. Certain stock imagery © Getty Images.

Print information available on the last page.

ISBN: 978-1-5043-9775-9 (sc)
ISBN: 978-1-5043-9776-6 (hc)
ISBN: 978-1-5043-9836-7 (e)

Library of Congress Control Number: 2018901986

Balboa Press rev. date: 02/26/2018

*To all my brilliant, star-eyed guides: eternal gratitude
for lifting my heart into symphony with yours.
To all the beautiful hearts in search of clarity: truth is simple
and easy to know. Allow yourself to know it. There is magic
awaiting at every step, and it's all yours to live it.*

I am enjoying this place I have reached: I love who I am, where I've been and who I am becoming.

The experience of being me and discovering my preferences each day is becoming more and more of a joy, delightful surprise and pleasure.

There is so much comfort and peace and loving strength for me in this being one with Myself. Self-criticism and self-doubt are gone, and in their place there is only light and clarity and loving growth, and a tremendous capacity to live life fully.

I recognize my path with ease, and decisions feel easy and inspired. If I sometimes seem to make mistakes or fail, I now remember instantly that there is no real mistake, nor failure. There is only exploration and feedback from life, and reaching forward, and every step along this path has its meaning, its purpose and its value.

The more I witness my potential revealing, the more it appears to grow and bloom even further and richer than I have ever imagined.

This harmony within translates into all areas of my life, and everything is unfolding with deliciously increasing ease and satisfaction.

Indeed, every day feels like magic and flow and brilliant clarity, every day feels like new blessings.

This is what it feels like, to live alive.

Contents

Introduction

"The real question is not whether life exists after death.
The real question is whether you are alive before death"
-Osho

Dear friend,

You are in for a roller coaster of discoveries and self-discoveries that are guaranteed to help you get powerful, condensed, applicable understanding. These are the kind of knowledge and tools that are vital for any human who wants to take control of their own life, and their ability to intentionally experience powerful freedom and joy, on a daily basis and not just once in a while.

This is the kind of profound and epic, life transforming understanding I wish I had already revealed inside my mind and heart as early as possible in my life. I instinctively searched for it throughout my childhood and younger years, and well into my adulthood, as we all probably do, whether we are aware of it or not.

These are powerful concepts and methods that I have experienced, studied, explored and tested on myself and hundreds of others over the past twenty years, often bruising my heart and tugging at my mind, often learning from the success of others, a few times seriously staggering, broken to pieces and ready to give up on myself and life as I knew it.

You don't want to go through life like this.

Enough billions have done it before us, haven't they?

You need a map and a solution, and you are ready for clarity, here and now.

We live in a brave new age, where people are less and less willing to settle for darkness and suffering as normality. I know you are no longer willing to settle, either. You've come too far and you have just had enough. You intuitively feel that this "reality" cannot be the whole story, and that the degree of suffering and injustice you perceive in your life and the world is not made for humans to endure. This is how I felt for so long, trapped in an existence with rules, premises and expectations impossible to tolerate for long. More often than not, life felt hard, it felt cruel, and very rarely made any sense.

You want to break through this haze and stop feeling powerless.

You want to be equipped with the understanding and tools that you need, in order to break through personal perceived limitations that have long stood between you and your full potential. Between you and constant, predictable joy, confidence, clarity and peace of mind. Because this is ultimately what we all want: to live alive and full of passion, every single day, in control of our experience, growing into the beautiful, colorful, vibrant, powerful giant butterflies we are meant to be.

Nobody wants to live life in grey. Nobody wants to go through life a raw, small and scared caterpillar, riding on a roller-coaster of emotions, sometimes up, sometimes deep in a dark pit of fear and despair, rarely enjoying fleeting moments of happiness or content, at the mercy of apparently random events that are hardly under your control.

Yet many of us stay stuck in the caterpillar mode for so long, for years, maybe for decades. In truth, many of us never bloom. Many of us die still a bud, unborn, blind and deaf and completely unaware of the divine, gigantic symphony that life actually is!

I feel the ultimate meaning of failure and tragedy is a life wasted; a greatness never lived; a human potential never explored or touched or developed.

Your life, lived small and guarded and insecure.

You, never daring to be the insanely beautiful and powerful divine flame that you could set ablaze right now, instead of living like a tiny, humble spark. What a tremendous loss, beautiful brave heart, the sadness of it always fills me up with tears!

Because I was you not very long ago.

I had always known deep inside – even as a small child- that I was meant for great things, and that our world is a magic, enchanted one. And as the years unfolded, my life seemed to wander so far away from that path of noble significance I knew I was made for, and the magic was fading away, to be felt very rarely. In my darkest moments I felt the deadening sadness: the tragedy of wasting **me.** The sadness of settling for so much less than I was meant to be, and settling for a strange world, devoid of all the joy and wonder and enchantment I had initially known.

The sadness of failing the plan I knew God had laid out for me.

This is not how you want to live until the end.

This book speaks to my younger self, my children, my dear friends and all of you, my loved ones of every age who feel something is missing: the puzzle of life just doesn't seem to fit together, things don't make sense and they just don't add up. You seem to be wandering your way through it, drifting –just like I used to- often without a compass to show the North of life, questioning the meaning of it all, and your purpose here.

When we lack this understanding – because it is all about understanding, clarity and awareness, we struggle like blind, ignorant bats in the open daylight. We are likely to draw bitter conclusions about how life works and what the world is all about. Disheartening, discouraging conclusions about our own role in it. This is one of the reasons depression is rampant on our planet and humans feel lonelier and more discouraged than ever, despite the wealth of communication channels available to all of us. We search for our meaning and a measure of our greatness in all the wrong places.

Breathe deeply, brave heart, you are not alone on this quest. Please feel my love, and the love of the many others going through the same transformations! We are there for real, in real time. Reach out to me any time and share your challenges and insights! I promise you will find a loving and patient supporter, one who fully understands what you are going through.

I have imagined this little book as a chain of logically structured chapters, a coherent sequence of steps, accompanied by exercises and examples, that guide you to experience a new understanding of yourself, our world and how to make the best of both.

My heart is on fire and ablaze with a prayer: the brightest vision of you, the free, powerful, wise and insanely joyful creator of this unique masterpiece that is you and your life. I know it is possible for you, because it was possible for me and for many others.

Let's rise.

Chapter 1

WHO DO YOU THINK YOU ARE?

When you look back upon your life, do you feel that you have been on an emotional roller coaster, with intervals of calm (when things were approximately fine and you felt approximately balanced), inevitably followed by inexplicable emotional lows and confidence decline, when everything seemed to fall apart, for no evident reason? And in those low moments, you couldn't seem to make any sense of life, the world and your own role in this complicated movie.

You find yourself feeling so deeply vulnerable, drifting, like a leaf in a whirlpool, fighting for direction, yearning for stability and quickly losing hope and your ability to trust yourself and the life around you.

This is true for what *my* life was, several years back.

I used to think joy, happiness, as well as enthusiasm, are either traits we are born with, or things that happen *to* us, at times and during circumstances I had no control over. I was fairly good at feigning confidence and optimism, but in reality I only had some random ideas on how to feel happy. None of these ideas were reliable, though, to produce happiness or at least a feeling of safety at predictable times, or when I needed them most. Also, if I happened to run across the big H, happiness, I had no idea how to make it last a bit longer, or how to enhance it, to feel it stronger.

While I had quite long intervals of positive in my career, relationships and emotional life- and apparently everything important was going on pretty well, I wasn't always able to see, to realize, to contemplate the goodness of it all, to take it all in and to actually enjoy it consistently. I would easily allow my focus to flow towards worrisome or fearful thoughts and I would eventually find myself again in a deep pit of discouragement, low confidence, pessimism and sadness.

And every time I found myself in this state again, I would curse my bad fortune and desperately wonder what was so fundamentally wrong with me? Was I inherently damaged in some dark, inexplicable way? "Why can't I just be fine with what I have, why all this internal turmoil? Will I ever, ever be all right - for good, or at least for a long, long time?"

I secretly started to believe I was a lost cause, damaged goods. I would cry against life and whoever made it all so hard to figure out, and I would once again lose trust and hope in my ability to ever be happy.

This all seemed to be complicated furthermore by the lack of a proper life map, some sort of clearly designed and explained guidance- answers about why we are here, what is the purpose of this world and my existence in it? What is of utmost importance, in our daily interactions, as well as for our entire lifespan?

What is the best way to live our lives? In accordance to whose definition of "best"?

I didn't seem to have a framework to refer to, in so many areas of my life – or the framework I had was not enabling me to stay consistently happy and confident. Quite the contrary. And this often left me feeling frustrated, discouraged and utterly out of control. Like a lost little fish, swimming through the random waves of a river, with no vision about its destination, and no power to make its way across the troubled, unpredictable waters.

You'd expect humanity to have come up with a clear, condensed and explicit manual for living by now.

You'd expect so many billions of lives and deaths to have been enough motivation for someone to finally step up and put together the whole puzzle, to select what matters most and make it understandable to even the most unsophisticated reader. So that the next generations don't have to wander around blindly, just like their ancestors before them, starting from the same starting line, reaching for the same known finish, trying to learn roughly the same lessons, going through the same tragedies, chasing the same illusions, making the same mistakes and living in the same haze and confusion, over and over again.

In fact, the truth and the answers have always been entirely available to us at all times, some in all the amazing books out there, some come through personal experience, mentors or —most powerfully — through pure, direct inspiration.

Often, however, you just feel like it will take forever to figure it all out. When we read a book, for example, (even the holy ones), the coins finally start to drop only by the third or fourth reading (if ever!). The language and examples are no longer adequate for our times, and those who offer to interpret them for you have their own human biases, beliefs and agendas, and this could just sink you further down in fear, guilt and shame. Not what you need.

You may run across people, relationships and events that throw you far, far away from your track, and confuse you even more. Or you get busy with life and lose track of your findings. You forget how much you wanted to find these answers. Until you hit the wall again. And let's be honest, when you're deep in the dark pit you rarely feel like reading one more book.

What on Earth are we supposed to do, then?

Wouldn't you wish you had a map? A little book that spells the rules of the game of life in very simple terms? Someone to connect the dots for you - not all of them, but at least enough dots to get yourself out of the pit forever and set in the right direction, with a working, understandable, applicable, easy to decipher recipe for happy life.

I had desperately yearned for, and searched for the same. Not that I was able to even formulate this need in my mind until a later stage, but I often felt like a stranger in the wrong movie. I felt that reality as I saw it just didn't make enough sense and there were many, *too many* pieces of my puzzle missing.

So I kept digging and searching, ever more frustrated. This feeling of being a misfit in a weird world was only getting stronger as I was growing up and facing all the hardships of the world – this is what we are taught: you have to grow up and take in all the fear, injustice and tough times of humanity and make them all your own. Toughen up. What a bunch of nonsense! That is humanly impossible, without tearing yourself apart! This is why people get sick, depressed and die. Really.

This book doesn't claim to have placed the whole puzzle together. But for my life and the lives of many friends it does seem to connect the most important parts of it, to build your better understanding, to take the leap from being a passive, insecure victim, to a powerful master of your own amazing destiny. And isn't this what we all crave for?

Overall my life had always been good. I had faced some challenges big and small, but I have almost always had love, health, and much more than my basic needs covered. Indeed, I would often look around at the less fortunate people, and beat myself down further for not being able to enjoy the happy life I had all reasons to live.

If I wasn't happy, I blamed myself for being unable to appreciate and live life fully.

If I found myself in those rare moments of happiness or peace, I quickly poisoned it myself with (useless) pieces of "wisdom", such as: nothing is supposed to last, and how could it last, since there are many others out there who are still suffering? This would normally suffice to immediately tone down my enthusiasm and bring me "down to earth" and "back to normal". Down to fear, sadness and grief, back into the pit.

It was as if an invisible force was determined to make sure I stay down. Play small. Fly low. Never allow me to fully live.

I felt like I was fighting a hopeless fight, against invisible cruel and powerful enemies I could neither see, nor understand.

It wasn't until much later that I realized I was fighting a mirror.

There was no enemy outside.

It had been me, doing this to myself, all along.

Another thing I didn't realize for very long was that all my extensive education, my multiple degrees, my speaking several languages – our conventional education up to this point– were no matching tools for my quest, and could never provide all the keys to understanding what you are going to understand here and now. They never taught me how to take control of my reality and how to harness happiness like a master.

I strongly believe in the power of education, and especially self-education. And I know that, as we speak, this knowledge and understanding becomes part of conventional education now. Great reason to celebrate already!

While life and our surrounding reality do provide us with challenges and good times as well, with ups and downs, I learnt there is a bulletproof way to increase your number of ups tremendously, and bounce back up from your downs in little or no time.

There is a sure, tested, older-than-the-worlds way to tune into this newfound power, build steam and gather momentum until you own it and it owns you. You become one and it becomes your dominant nature. And then there is no way back.

A precious golden tip that you will find repeated in this book: throughout the process, the key to getting the most out of it is in *being very gentle* with yourself: give yourself the time, the patience and kindness you would allow a five year old child, or your best friend. Give this newfound understanding the chance to sink in and permeate your consciousness, and as it does, you will start seeing tremendous changes in your external world as well.

Because this book is about *you*, and getting *you* to *become* the fully confident person you were born to be, let us start with a short and very powerful exercise. You will keep getting these along the way, as we know now that only information that you act upon is real power, and knowledge is no use unless you can remember it. Best way to remember things is by doing them, right?

Who do you think you are?

Who are you? Please answer this question in as many words as you want.

No clues provided for very good reasons, so bear with me and plunge into the answer: who are you?

I am

Chapter 2

YOUR PRIMARY IDENTITY

Do you remember the times when you were thirteen or fourteen, a teenager just blooming and getting a glimpse of "grown up life"? The roller coaster of emotions, the hopes, the insecurity and self-doubt, the ever-changing and challenging environment of your life, your feelings, your relations?

They all say the teenage years are tough, and that it all gets better as you grow older. And it does. Or so it should.

Yet once in a while, even in your life as a "mature, responsible, knowledgeable, grown up", you find yourself falling back into that state of raw, vulnerable, bewildered, confused, tear-filled eyed, trembling voice, completely soul-bare state of total uncertainty. AGAIN. Not a simple, short lived, fugitive sadness, but the kind of all-crushing pain that starves your heart and mind until you just forget who you are, and what a normal day looks like.

You feel like you are once again in the middle of nowhere, feeling like a nobody, a damaged life, bound to fail. A lost cause. A worthless shape with no essence.

And you cry out loud in the lonely depths of your mind "Ohhh, please, not again! I thought I was over all that! Oh, the horror of it all. Does it ever, ever go away *for good*? Am I *ever* going to be normal, confident and *stay* confident?!"

Yes, dear friend, I have been there too. I've been down, and up, and deep, deep down again, just like you.

So in the light of this apparent everlasting instability, how can you ever rely and trust that confidence is there to stay, yours to keep?

Whom and what can you actually ever count on being there to support you, at any time and forever?

Confidence comes from the certainty of knowing who you are and staying grounded in that, every day, every hour.

And who are you really? Why are you here? What is the purpose of it all? Why all the struggle and the hustle and the hard work, if all seems bound to crash once in a while anyway, all heading for a finish line we all know too well?

Stay with me while we explore this, I promise it lays the most solid ground for the rest of your life, once and for all.

You are an infinite divine joyful presence in a beautifully working human body. You and universal intelligence are not separated, but existing in a continuum. Solidity is only a matter of perception – science backs it up and every ancient wisdom and holy scripture confirms it, we will explore this too, shortly (I come with scientific proof, so stay with me please).

This is your first identity, your true nature. Free, joyful, peaceful, a powerful creator playfully at work, constantly expanding reality.

Everything else is secondary and temporary. Your roles as a son or daughter, sister or brother, wife or husband, girlfriend, mother, father, friend, career man or woman, artist, and so on are all just that: roles, beautiful and challenging and fun in themselves, but in continuous change and transformation.

Bare with me for a few minutes, this is really hot stuff and totally life-changing when you grasp its importance. I say, without any shadow of a doubt: if you understand this, everything else is implementation detail!

The ultimate goal and meaning of our lives is to create in a state of joy, love, gratitude, peace, excitement, resourcefulness, tolerance and inspiration, while experimenting with the challenges and wonders of various life situations, growing our full potential, developing and enjoying our talents and what the ancients called "virtues".

Really?

YES, yes and again yes.

Joy, freedom and a sense of perfect fulfillment define our natural state, the state that we are born in, one that we do not need to earn, nor deserve. A state where we feel powerful, generous and loving. The place from where we own the universal creative forces, the way *we* want it.

Love is the force that keeps the universe together, the essence of life. This is the reason why we always, always crave for love one way or another: this is the true nature of our being, and we are permanently drawn to it. If you dig deep down behind all our actions, even behind the darkest and most evil, at the bottom of them all there is an overwhelming need to be loved, connected, acknowledged, seen, validated, accepted, recognized, appreciated, wanted, admired and treasured. By ourselves, by others, by what we consider a higher power.

How comfortable are you with the concept of a universal intelligence that runs all things, a higher power, divine force, God, the good, the one that beats your heart and operates your trillions of cells – each a universe on its own? The all-pervasive force that made the Sun, the Universe, our astounding, infinitely diverse and ever-changing world. Call it what you like. I will call it God sometimes because it's shorter, but you can call it whatever you like (just call it!)

I do not aim to make you a believer, and I do not represent any religious affiliation in particular (they all lead to the same source).

What I deeply yearn for, my dearest wish is for you to claim and take the power and the life of abundance that are rightfully yours. For you to stand in full ownership of who you truly are. The stunning master of your faith and of your world.

These days more and more people have become familiar with the idea of the 'God within', an idea that is thousands of years old, but we are only understanding it literally now. Some of us know it with our logic and interpret it to be a metaphor of some sort. And some of us live it as a reality, in our hearts and minds and bodies and relationships with ourselves and others.

The Bible repeatedly tells us that we are a temple for God's spirit, and both ourselves and our bodies are sacred.

I am not preaching and I do not belong to a sect, as I said, neither do I aim to establish one. But I do know for a fact, however, that when you understand exactly who you are, in relation to this higher power and our world, there is no way you can go back to living in fear and doubt again. Never. You will know a different reality and you will own it once and for all.

In Hinduism's principal holy text the Bhagavad Gita we have the Krishna within, while the Koran tells us that Allah is closer than our jugular vein. The Buddhist scriptures talk about the Buddha within and correspondingly the Adi Granth, the Sikh holy text, describes that the one God is all pervading and alone dwells in the Mind.

Although many spiritual people are familiar with the idea that God is to be found within them, too, they often imagine that this is just symbolism, or some sort of small, divided piece of Divinity, or perhaps just some aspect of it reflected within us.

A fuller understanding often comes with experience. When you have lived this, nothing and nobody can take it away from you. When you acknowledge the infinity of power, the Creator within, you have made the ultimate and most important breakthrough.

I am not asking you to believe me – I understand that some of us find it difficult to accept something that they have not yet experienced with their senses – not that they are aware of it, actually. We are raised and trained to rely solely on the feedback we receive from our senses: the world we see, hear, smell, taste and touch.

But what about the music playing on your radio? Can you actually see the radio waves coming from the station and into your radio receiver? And yet you rely on your machine to give you music and the voices of the DJs without questioning the way it comes to you. Every time you speak on your mobile phone, you are certain that there is a connection between you and the other person, although you cannot see it.

You are completely willing to trust mobile phones, radio waves, the Wi-Fi, microwave ovens, the GPS system in your car to do their job. You know they are there, although you cannot see them. You put your life in the hands of unseen forces when you

travel by plane: they are guided by similar mechanisms. You trust them, because humans have found a way to understand, harvest, employ, coerce, and use forces that they cannot see, hear, smell, taste nor touch. But they have observed their effects and understood their laws and harnessed them for humanity's benefit.

What have you got to lose by trying this one too, then: reach out within the apparent loneliness inside your heart and mind. You think you are alone in there, don't you? Speak to this space for the next seven days (come on, you can do it, if you can listen to voices coming from your car's radio, without seeing the people behind them). Ask this space to make its presence felt to you, in a way that you can clearly perceive with your senses and emotions. Ask it to surface in your thoughts and….just relax. Relax as much as you can. Breathe deeply a few times and try to have as much fun and joy as you can. Do this as often as you can over the course of seven days. Come on, my friend, just seven days. I am already having loving fun at your expense, I am already seeing your face, when you stop dead in your tracks. When you get it.

Some people discover it through meditation or prayer. Myself, I took the biblical promise literally at some point, the promise where everything I'd ask for would be given. I asked, again and again for clarity and guidance and awareness. Do not imagine that I was in any way more enlightened than you are, I was just very desperate!

You see, this thing or force you will discover residing within is your first identity, your true nature, while everything else is secondary and temporary.

Why is this so crucially important?

Because everything else fluctuates and transforms permanently: your body, your mind, your emotions and your thoughts, your life and your abilities, your friends, family, your health, your looks, your wealth and career. In the physical world, change and transformation rule and this is the certainty. In the midst of uncertainty, the God or the Power Within You is the only immovable, unquestionable, invariable reality.

In my worst times of darkness, as well as in my brightest days, this presence and this powerful connection have been my rock, my never-hesitating, strongest friend and ally. When you reach within, when you are able to discern this voice from the rest – from your thoughts and your emotions – when you have strengthened it enough, you will own unparalleled levels of peace, confidence, joy, wisdom and clarity.

I say, without any shadow of a doubt, that once you understand and feel yourself supported and loved beyond imagination, every single day, you will never feel alone again. Never again deserted, powerless or desperate. When you have felt it for that just one second, there is no way back. No more wandering. You will know where you are going at any time and an ocean of love, confidence and abundance is going to open, right then and right there at your fingertips. Just ask.

You can reach out to this universal benevolent loving power at any moment in the day or night. You don't need to find it only in a church, a temple or a mosque. God is with you and all around you. Ask for what you need, and give thanks. Dwell on the feeling of gratitude and on the image of your dreams come true, for your prayers are coming to fruition much sooner when you can feel and see yourself there already. And they will unfold in ways that satisfy you far beyond what you expected.

I find this realization amazingly liberating. Knowing and experiencing ourselves as part of God anchors us in a much deeper reality. One where all fears and worries vanish, just like darkness when you turn on the light, since you know and feel it in your gut- that you are permanent, you are loved and protected, and you are enough. Not just sometimes, but every hour and every day of your life.

You are always the one in charge. It has always been you. You created the pleasant and unpleasant things in your life. You ask and the universe responds. You ask through the way you feel, which is a result of the thoughts and beliefs and images we entertain and focus on most of the time.

With this comes the understanding that living with joy and satisfaction on a daily basis is not wishful thinking, or unrealistic. It becomes achievable, normal and desirable, and it doesn't need justification or validation, or an excuse. In fact, it becomes evident that living in any other way is a proof of negligence, ignorance, lack of discipline. If you want to work hard at something, work hard at disciplining your thoughts, at redirecting them as often as it takes from the unwanted to your dreams and goals. From unpleasant to joyful, hopeful, constructive and positive.

You are officially free to be unapologetically strong, happy and confident for good.

You do not owe it to anyone to dim your light; to suffer; to play small. If you keep doing it, it will be your choice – but you will be a giant, pretending not to know it, trying to act as a dwarf. Imagine Superman and Wonder woman crawling and pretending to be babies.

What if you do not believe in God, or in a force for the good, waiting to support and shelter you? What if you had disappointments so large, what if sorrow and darkness surround you on a daily basis? What then?

Well, you always have the free choice of what to think and believe. Always. But let me ask you, at this point where everything seems lost anyway, what have you got to lose if you believe? If you reach within and beyond, when you need protection, love and confirmation that you will be all right?

There are so many ways you can do this. And there are so many reasons why you should do this, so much to gain.

You know what? Do not take my word for granted. Do not, in fact, take anyone's word for granted. Try. Try it for seven days, or try it for a month. Take God for a test drive: for a while, live as if you are Divinely protected and guided.

For seven days, every morning, every evening and every time you can remember, do any and all of these:

Feeling Power Prayer:

At any time, and especially before you start your day, talk to your heart, or to nature, and summon God and the Archangels, or the good powerful energies that inspire you, that you can relate to. Ask them for what you want, for guidance, support and protection. Ask for friends, for abundance and for love to come from all directions, and find the feeling place of this new reality, of the comfort and safety of knowing that help is on the way. Imagine how it feels to have these things come true, and maintain this feeling at high intensity as much as you can. Feeling is key with prayer and creation of a new reality. Your mind does not know the difference between reality and imagination, and a powerful, emotionally reinforced image will set the Creator Within you at work. And the Creator knows no limits, except the limits you set.

How do you know that you feel your Inner Essence, that you are one with It? A few examples from my own life:

- When you listen to your favorite music and your hearts soars like a kite on a sunny, windy vortex, higher and higher. This is you feeling God within.

- When you drive your car with the same favorite music on, and you are overtaken by the most amazing sense of freedom, support and power. There is so much beauty and goodness that you feel larger than life, and the most noble sense of greatness surfaces from somewhere deep inside you. You experience what feels like magic, supernatural ideas and beautiful visions of things that matter much to you, and you find yourself simply *knowing*, with certainty and solid confidence, without the faintest shadow of a doubt, that what you feel and think is real, valid, true and valuable. This is you feeling God within.

- When you hold your newborn child in your arms for the first time (or when you think of anyone in high appreciation) and you feel like your eyes bloom in flowers of light, beaming the most adoring energy on others, and all your inside feels like molten honey rivers of happy music from another world. This is you feeling God within.

- When you support someone in need, you experience their relief and you acknowledge your own goodness. Time seems to stand still, and your reality transforms for moments into an overwhelming feeling that all is well, and that you are so powerfully good and worthy that you are perfectly golden. This is you feeling God within.

Anchor and Expand Yourself:

In the temple of your own mind, reach out and visualize an imaginary light that connects you to the Sun in the sky, as well as to a deep place inside our Earth. Bring this bright, hot liquid light into your heart and breathe it in, and expand it beyond your body, beyond your house, beyond your city, beyond your country and our planet. It takes a few seconds and it works whether you believe in it, or not. Just do it. From this expanded state, ask for all that you want. It is not just your imagination, I guarantee, although all you have to do is imagine, sense or feel. Ask and be grateful, for it is coming your way.

Loving Heart Communion:

Put your hands on your solar plexus and your heart. Breathe gently in and out, slowly. Tell your heart continuously "I love you. I love you. I love you." Whenever you feel scared, angry, desperate, helpless, upset or alone, this will work wonders. Keep doing it for as long as it takes you to feel better, it may take two minutes in the beginning; with little practice you will achieve your peace in seconds.

Several years ago, I lost a pregnancy. It was a deeply painful time in my life. I felt guilty, I felt empty. I felt lost. Nothing could heal the darkness inside my heart. And it grew darker every day, until I could no longer sleep at night. I would lie in bed, wide awake, a wave of sheer terror going throughout my body and my heart, drowning my soul and starving any little hope I had left. Nothing I had been trying for days was helping. It was as if a mad, terrifying force had taken over the theater of my mind, and was playing havoc with my feelings. I was in hell, no doubt about it.

As I knew from my life before this, there is only one place to turn to, when nobody or no thing can help you any longer. **It was God**

and the commitment to be there for myself, come what may, to stand in there where nobody else could stand with me, to hold my own hand and heal my own life, no matter what. No matter what, it was just me and Me.

I said a quick prayer, a hot, heartfelt, desperate prayer, like I said so many in my life before. In an instant, in a blink of an eye I had a glimpse of inspiration: I said to myself "I will never leave you, no matter what happens to us, I am here with you." I felt inspired to rest my hands on my heart and keep saying "I love you". It took perhaps one minute, and a complete sense of peace, sweet, heart healing peace took over me. And it stayed. It washed away the fear, the guilt, the panic and the anguish.

Who was talking to the terrified me? Who was comforting me? Who was taking over? My conscious mind was fully absorbed and paralyzed by fear, I promise you. My heart was crying in total agony, unable to move one inch towards a better feeling, hard as I tried. These parts of me that I was consciously aware of – they were shackled. But the God within, our soul, the divine part of us is always aware that we are on some level always safe, immortal, and that nothing can actually harm us when we are connected in that way. All we have to do is call and ask, and the calls of love and gratitude are the ones that will connect you almost instantly to Who you really are.

This is the part of you that is larger than life, everlasting, always powerful, loving, inspired and noble; as you get in touch with it more often, this permanent nature inside of you takes over and drives your perception and your existence up and beyond, to a whole new dimension, while you still go out and about your daily life. Yet your life will be completely changed.

If I had to choose one thing, and one only, that will always, always take your heart out of sorrow, no matter how deep, this is the one: feeling a deep commitment, love, compassion and gratitude for yourself - deciding and promising yourself that you will never, ever again abandon yourself, no matter what.

No matter how tough things seem, you always have *I LOVE YOU*.

I am talking to you and I stand grounded in a truth that is a daily reality for me. I live this every single day. This is the power that carries me, guides me and blesses my life and my heart every moment. *All I ever did was not give up. I just kept coming back to it again and again, building this reality and practice into my life until it became intertwined with a vast majority of my moments.* I bless myself and my loved ones, dear mentors, friends, strangers in the street; I bless my day and my work, I bless everything whenever I remember, and it became a habit, a way of life. And in exchange my life is blessed as a whole.

Ask Archangel Michael or Jesus or your favorite Guide to open your senses, so that you can see, feel, hear, understand and speak the truth and reality at all times, to be able to perceive and sense God, or your higher power guidance at any minute.

You need this because there are a lot of illusions woven into our reality, due to our perceptions, beliefs and understanding, and we need help discerning illusion from reality, especially when we are "down". We want clarity.

This works even if you don't believe it fully. All you need to do is ask.

Archangels, these amazing beings, are just another expression of God's presence in our midst, ready to step in and lend a hand.

You do not disturb them and any benign request (that doesn't hurt anyone) will be received with joy and eagerness.

Try. These are simple, powerful, tested solutions with no side effects whatsoever.

I have many true stories to share with you, about how this amazing loving intelligence responds and shapes my reality. About "signs", angels and apparently impossible events.

I love my grandparents dearly and I have been blessed to know so much love from them, that it lights up my life to this day, years after they passed away. You see, love lasts longer than gold or the rocky mountains, it burns like a bonfire in the night of our fears, rekindling our hearts, showing the way to hope, bliss and beyond.

My grandfather passed away during the cold month of January. It was one of the coldest times of the year in Romania.

Now I knew this moment would come, I had prepared for it for as long as I can remember, and this meant making sure he knows he is deeply loved, cherished and taken care of. Yet when the day came, I found myself yearning for the certainty that he continues to exist in some form or another, beyond the grave, beyond the remains of a lifeless body that he inhabited for almost ninety-three years.

Loved ones transitions can sink your hearts and minds into despair, if you are not conscious of who we are. The perceived loss in itself is painful and dramatic enough sometimes to kneel the strongest hearts. But my worst fear, one that would have debilitated me if I didn't know better, was that I had lost him forever. That I would never, ever have him near again.

The day after the funeral I was sitting alone by his grave; it was early January, a cold, cloudy, Transylvanian winter in this little village among the hills.

The doubt was creeping in on me and wrapping its frozen fingers around my heart.

So I did what I always do.

I asked. I asked with full passion that if he continues to exist, I need a sign. A clear, unmistakable message.

And the message came, clearly, as it always does.

In the midst of cold winter, a gentle rain shower started. And within minutes all the clouds were gone, and a beautiful rainbow spanned the innocent countryside!

The temperature was just a few degrees above zero. But the probability of it happening, right then, right there, was below zero. Statistically speaking.

This is not a story, it really happened. And it is just one of countless apparently inexplicable and unlikely events in my life.

I hope I am reaching through to you, it would mean so much to me to know that I have inspired one heart, encouraged one soul to reach out and within, and to count on Help to be there. To never feel alone or helpless again.

Do you remember the exercise you did in the previous chapter, where you told me about you, and who you are. How did you identify yourself? What defines you: your name, your age, your role as a woman or man, perhaps a parent or a spouse? A career-driven person? An optimistic and ambitious one?

Are any of these anything more than roles? Wonderful roles that we are all called to fulfill during our lifetimes. I hope today you will add one more powerful role to your identity. The most powerful role, I believe. Your only permanent one: a divine being, in a human body.

All right, you are an intelligent person and you probably also need science and proof to back up this whole story, before you can accept it and incorporate it into your own identity and into your reality.

So did I, and I got all proof and readings in the world that I could get my hands on over the past twenty years. I still do, I still need every question answered, but everything has become so, so much easier these days.

The science part is coming.

But I need to tell you, reading, thinking and the mind only gets one part of the deal for us: there is a point where we need to start living, feeling, experiencing and absorbing everything through our senses and more.

Hang in there, my wise and patient friend, it gets more "real" and clear as we progress along this journey.

Until then, do start any and all of the above tools I just shared. It only takes few minutes of your time, but done daily and several times a day, they are total game changers. They brought powerful progress for me and for everyone who employs them.

Go ahead right now. You will see and feel immediate changes. Start with five minutes for each prayer, meditation or exercise and as you get comfortable with it, you can reduce or expand the time. I may spend five seconds or five minutes on the same prayer, on different days, as I need. Take it easy and make it a priority to just be awake and peaceful within.

My reminder: give yourself the patience, love and understanding that you need, as you would to a five-year old child.

At the end, write down how you feel afterwards, and what has come up for you (because the more you practice, you will notice very interesting things coming up: flashes of inspiration, ideas, feelings, images and so on, each and every one of us will experience it differently).

Anchor and Expand Yourself

Feeling Power Prayer

Loving Heart Communion

Chapter 3

SCIENCE: YOUR THOUGHTS AND YOUR EMOTIONS, THE POWERFUL CONNECTORS

You have come to know that lasting confidence can only be rooted in a clear understanding of who we are, and how we function. This is why it is definitely worth taking a look at the way our bodies, our minds and our emotions are constructed. To understand their roles and how they can become our beloved partners, instead of our controlling masters.

Everything is made up of energy.

Energy is a concept used by both science and spiritual authors over the years and it is (finally!) accepted to mean the same thing. There is nothing surreal about it, nor is it just some hippie psychobabble, when you understand it clearly. Energy simply is. What we used to define as solid matter is energy as well, energy whose frequency is so low that our senses can perceive it.

Your body is made of energy, your fingers and the book or the device they hold as you read, the air you breathe, the chair or couch you are sitting on, the waves received as sound by your ears, and the particles translated into light and visual images by your eyes and your brain.

Solidity is an illusion created by our senses, senses that are not fine enough to perceive reality in all its full, infinitely complex and minute details. And thank God we are made so, it would be extremely tiresome for our conscious minds to constantly have to deal with the trillions of events that happen within and around us in every moment, from sub atomic level to the entire fabric of reality (light, sounds, movement, speed, color, bodily functions, like breathing and blood circulation and so on). While our conscious mind is selective in terms of where it shifts its focus, this selectiveness is in great part controlled by the patterns already existent in our subconscious mind: the grand computer behind the scenes, the powerful immense storage of all the data that we have ever come across in our existence.

To have a visual grasp of this huge reality that exists without our senses being able to detect it, we can imagine the wheels of a car in motion, or a fidget spinner in our hands. Their spinning at high speed creates the illusion of solidity: our eyes perceive both the car wheel and the fidget spinner as full discs, and can no longer see the empty space within the spokes of the wheel, or the arms of the fidget spinner respectively. The same goes for the movement of electrons around the nucleus of an atom; they are constantly spinning at very high speed, and, in simple terms, our bodies and everything that we call matter is made up of trillions and trillions of such lively, busy particles.

Yes, there is permanent movement within ourselves, our bodies, and our surrounding world. The term *vibration* or *frequency* refers to the speed of those electrons spinning round their atom's nucleus, and then moving in a permanent exchange with the other atoms, cells, organs and so on. Apart from the nucleus and electrons, there is a lot of apparent void inside the atom, more than ninety percent. Imagine an empty football stadium (the atom), and the little ball at the center (the nucleus) and you have a fair image of these sub-atomic proportions. But void is very much alive with information, and the atoms that make up the people and our surroundings are in constant communication. We are all interconnected, and permanently exchanging, with each other and the world around us.

Going back to our minds and our emotions, the powerful connectors that take energy and shape it into our realities, just like the sculptor takes a marble block, or a ball of clay, and shapes it into a beautiful statue, or a terrible mess. We constantly create through our thoughts – our focus on and attention to things, ideas, memories, events, people, and qualities. The symptom of a thought, a beam of photons running through our body is an emotion.

Dr Jill Bolte Taylor, Harvard-trained neuroscientist, had the amazing opportunity (yes, opportunity, as she recovered and is back to tell the tale) of having a brain stroke herself. She experienced her own mind (the analytical, left-brain part of it) deteriorate within hours. She gives the most vivid description of what it feels like to live from your right side of the brain. Describing the different functions of our brain's right and left hemispheres, she explains how the right side intakes information, in the form of energy, through all our physical senses, and constantly compounds it into this fabulous canvass that we perceive as our present moment.

As her logical, analytical left side of the brain went into temporary shut down, she experienced herself as the energy being that we all are, connected to one other and the entire existence. United in an infinite, expanding continuum, that takes our humanity and the whole of life ever forward, its beauty and variety unfolding without end.

Please take fifteen minutes and watch Dr Taylor's presentation "My stroke of insight" on TED.com. It is the best word description of someone's coming into the full awareness of who we are. Not just a logical, theoretical awareness, but one that is lived and perceived through all our available senses and levels of consciousness. She brilliantly illustrates how, in any given moment, we can perceive ourselves as a seamless part of the continuum of existence, or as separate entities.

Dr Taylor experienced the human level version of what quantum physics records at sub-atomic level in the Heisenberg Uncertainty Principle: a particle can exist simultaneously as a particle and a wave, until the observer's attention causes it to "collapse" into one or the other.

In other words, **the fabric of our reality is one of sheer unlimited potential, and our attention to, and focus on it constantly shapes and molds it into being.**

Furthermore, we are all connected and we all influence our world.

"Everything that you will ask in prayer, believing, you will receive."
Mark 21:22 (The Bible – Aramaic Bible in Plain English)

We have all heard these reassuring words at some point or another, but the reason many of us fail to see the results of prayer or meditation, the fulfillment of our desires, is that we don't know where the focus is in this sentence.

Yet all successful people have come to master this principle and use it in their favor, whether they consciously know it or not. That is the part with "believe that you have received it". In other words, to already live its certainty in your mind: the reality of your accomplished dreams and desires. To make yourself believe in the inevitability of it. To literally rely on it, and peacefully count on it to be done. To feel the feeling of it in your heart, in your body, because your thoughts and your feelings are the sparks that ignite the fire and bring your dreams to fruition. The fisherman that throws the net far and beyond, to bring in the delicious catch.

Once you figure out what our reality is made up of, it becomes evident that we are not helpless victims in our own life movie, to whom life just happens.

You begin to understand your true role and the immense impact you can have at any time on your life.

Yes, you, dear friend, can, at any given moment, be an active and powerful creator, instead of a passive, apparently hopeless little wheel in the larger machinery of life.

You can, at any time, step into the full feeling of who you really are, and what amazing magic you can work at the snap of your fingers (or with a snap of good mind work!).

You are an infinite Divine presence in a beautifully working body. You and this positive force, or energy, are not separated, but existing in a continuum.

We already know now that everything in our reality, all "matter" is made up of energy. Matter seen under a very powerful microscope shows you molecules and atoms and then you can observe the tiniest particles of matter at work, electrons and photons, particles and waves.

This is true for the chair you sit in, a book, the radio waves, the air you breathe, and it's true for your body. Everything in this world is made up of energy, and at microscopic level you could see that inside atoms there is a lot of apparently empty space, in reality alive with information. This is the fabric of our reality. Solidity is an illusion, your body and the whole world around you are just trillions of trillions of atoms held together in electromagnetic fields.

Do you begin to see the implications of this? I still remember the first time I grasped this concept, my jaw dropped and my heart was in awe at the miracle that this whole universe and we are. And I was finally free to allow spirituality and science to embrace and melt into each other for eternity. What a relief! Thank goodness we live in these times: five hundred years ago people were tortured, burned and killed for entertaining such concepts! When we look at history, we realize how far we have come, and that we now stand in a much better world than hundreds of generations before us.

The world, including ourselves, is an endless ocean of interconnected energy, in which we –through our conscious minds - are Powerful Creators.

Another beautiful and clear illustration of *the influence our mind has on creating "external" reality* can be found in Dr Masaru Emoto's research, condensed in his book, The Hidden Messages of Water. Emoto's studies prove that thoughts and feelings affect physical reality. He presented intentions to the water, in the shape of spoken words, music or written labels, and then photographed the changes in the shape of the frozen water crystals.

He found that water from clear springs, and water that has been exposed to loving words shows brilliant, complex, and colorful patterns, much like perfect, intricate snowflakes. In contrast, polluted water, or water exposed to negative thoughts, forms incomplete, chaotic, asymmetrical patterns, with dull colors.

The main implications are extremely powerful, and create a new understanding of how we can positively (or negatively) impact our own health and the world around us. We are just beginning to crack the door open into a larger, much clearer perception of the stuff we and the universe are made of. Great, amazing times lie right ahead of us!

One other pioneer of our times, cell biologist Bruce Lipton, further documents the power of mind over matter and the *shaping influence that our thoughts and emotions have over our physical body and health.*

In his "Biology of Belief" he explains in scientific terms and great detail that genes do not really control our lives, as it was previously thought after the discovery of the DNA. He proves that the nucleus is not the "brain" of the cell as it was thought for decades, but the gonad needed for reproduction (even if their nuclei and genes are removed, cells can survive for up to two months or more. They continue to exhibit complex, coordinated, life-sustaining behaviors, but eventually die, not because they have lost their brains, but because they have lost their ability to reproduce and are unable to replace failed proteins or replicate themselves).

Lipton shows that the true brain controlling cellular life is the cell's membrane, a skin with multiple permeable layers that holds the contents of a cell together. The cell's operations are not controlled by DNA blueprints stored in the nucleus, as we used to be told. Instead, Lipton demonstrates that the cell membrane contains receptors and proteins whose function is to receive information from the environment, and send it to the cell nucleus, where proteins controlling DNA use the information to turn DNA on or off. And this, in turn, completely changes millions of commands that literally transform our physical bodies, for better or worse.

In simple terms, your environment (and interpretation of it) changes your body. Your environment is made up not only of the apparently solid physical reality factors, such as temperature, your diet, the air your breathe, how much you exercise, etc. What is also extremely relevant is your interpretation of your environment, your learned reactions to it, that further branch into your thoughts and their attached feelings.

Knowing that you are a Powerful Creator and that you shape reality through your thoughts, the next question comes naturally.

Chapter 4

WHAT ARE YOU DOING HERE? YOUR PURPOSE AND LIFE MISSION

QUIZ time: Please describe your purpose in life in five paragraphs or more. You can write right here and now. You want to touch upon questions such as:

Why am I living in this world?

What gives meaning to my life?

At age 100, looking back, what should I have done or become, to feel that my life has been worth living (so far)?

What would I want to do, if time, money, health were not an issue, if I had no restrictions whatsoever? What "crazy", "big" dreams would I go for?

I always look forward to learning about other people's dreams with excitement and anticipation, as there is always gold hidden in people's perceptions and aspirations. I believe every one of us is a teacher and a model for others, with a unique view and experience, with something special to share.

Dreams, goals, objectives, desires, are fascinating. Because if we pursue them in the right way, they shape our life. They fill it up with meaning and they make us feel alive, powerful artists, creating our own unique, beautiful masterpiece.

The trouble is, as you already know, that the vast majority of people go through life enslaved by fears, kneeling under perceived obligations, those "musts" and "shoulds" and "cannots" they picked up from their families, from society, from the conclusions they draw after their own personal experiences.

They build up walls and limitations and they often abandon their dreams in favor of "practicality" and "common sense" and "decency". They do not act unless they have validation and approval from family or peers. They hope and wait for someone to give them permission to live life the way they want it. This permission rarely comes as such, and in the meantime you actually forget about the life you wanted in the first place.

You give up on your dreams – and on yourself- much, much too soon. And that is a sad, sad thing, so many beautiful masterpieces never born to see the light.

Do not feel intimidated if you haven't figured it out yet. When you hear people saying that they have a clear life purpose, please remember that this clarity rarely came over night, it is more of a gradual revelation.

To illustrate, I would love to share with you about my own life purpose, and how I became increasingly aware of it as I sifted and stumbled through various life experiences.

It has always been a background feeling, a subtle thought, but I came to know it with certainty at some point. I started jotting down notes and key words and qualities and soon enough I knew it clearly.

I have always felt I wanted to help and give support and hope, encourage and uplift, starting with family and loved ones, and moving further outwards, to reach as many people as possible. A great twist, a revelation came for me when I understood that my own joy, my own happiness, my own strong connection with a higher power for the good, will be the key to fulfilling my dream. My purpose.

Just like many others, I used to live with various expectations about what life, relations, success and love should look and feel like. I had my own little unconscious blueprint about what family should be. And then a whole chain of events started demolishing my whole domino kingdom: down went family, out the window all the money, freedom over, love imploded on itself, health collapsing, several of my close relations burning in the flames of conflict, fear and resentment. And at the bottom of it all I found myself, an apparent failure (in my own eyes), in midst of a reality that had no resemblance to what I knew or imagined before. Nothing seemed to fit the plan I had for my life.

Looking back, I see the movie of it, like a slow motion, incredibly perfect drama, the madness of which only I could feel. Knowing that we are the architects of our own lives now allows me to see how I triggered the apparent mayhem onto myself. I understand that it was necessary for me to lose it all (in my perception), so that I could face my true power. So that I could step forward and take ownership of Who I really am. Who we all are.

When we look carefully, we find that the solutions, the required skills and answers were actually there already, gently laid in our hands months and years before the actual crisis. For example, I had read Louise Hay's "You Can Heal Your Life" months before my life started falling into pieces. I met amazing therapists and doctors months before I needed them, or right around the time. It looks like there is an invisible puppet master, setting up the stage for us.

The puppet master is none other than yourself.

In the strongest contrast there is often great growth awaiting. The gold I found in midst of my own crisis was the confirmation that our purpose here is to live joyfully, while expanding and contributing to the wellness and happiness of others.

And our joy, wellbeing, fulfillment and progress are our own responsibility. Relying on, and expecting other people to make us happy is the recipe for disaster that has kept humanity in suffering for millennia. It is unrealistic to expect another human being to be constantly dedicated to finding out and delivering what makes me happy. Some of the bravest of us have tried to make others happy, to find out, always, that it is mission impossible. For the simple reason that we cannot manage and control the inner life of another, and happiness is all about inner management, the ability to appreciate, trust and enjoy yourself and your own life.

Joy. Happiness. Hope. Freedom. Confidence. They are powerful states of consciousness.

Your direction in life is an end result of your thought process, of your emotional framework, of your decisions, and ultimately of your actions.

Your actions and choices determine your life. We can all relate to this. Just look ten or twenty years back and think of a decision you could have made differently? A different school than the one you chose? Another life partner? What would your life be like today? Better, worse, or just different? You see the point.

And if we take a closer look at what determines your actions, it will look like this:

Beliefs/Thoughts → Emotions → INNER STATE → Decisions → Actions = DIRECTION OF OUR PHYSICAL LIFE

What determines your choices is the emotional state you are in, the way you feel about yourself and your world in the present moment, coupled with your knowledge - both conscious and intuitive.

Your thoughts and emotions are the power engines that make up (or break down) your state and your perception of reality in the present moment.

In any moment we experience emotions, even when we are completely at peace inside. **Any emotion we experience is, in fact, the rich collage or canvas of our life in that particular moment.**

Our emotional state (our feelings and perceptions) has a tremendous influence on our decisions, on the way we approach reality and people in our life. And yes, decisions (or lack thereof) influence the trajectory of our actions, and literally steer our life in one direction or another, upstream or downstream.

Have you noticed that when you are well rested, in good physical shape, happy about your life and yourself, connected to your Higher Power in a conscious way, you tend to be more generous; more optimistic; more resourceful and successful; more resilient. Obstacles seem no big deal. This is surely true for me and my life.

On the other hand, when you are not well physically, emotionally, mentally, when you are out there deaf and blind and unaware of the God within, any small event looks a tragedy and a pending disaster. There is loom and doom at every turn, treachery and malice in everyone's face and in their words.

As we have previously seen, there is plenty of research nowadays that shows how the way we see events and the world, our perceptions, determine our behavior (and rewrites our DNA).

The way we see the world, ourselves, people and events around us, the meaning and interpretations that we give to things are constructions based on **beliefs.** Beliefs are Conclusions and References that we have learned and absorbed from our families and society, or derived from our personal experiences.

For example, most kids are not very fond of doctors, since they associate doctors with vaccines, needles and pain; they believe doctor's visits must be dreadful experiences to some degree. To illustrate a different perception, coming from a different experience, my kids are blessed enough to have grandpa as their doctor, so their associations and beliefs about doctors are completely different. Their experience with doctors, hospitals and needles is not exactly a happy one, but not a fearful one either.

Since beliefs are such powerful filters, colored lenses through which we perceive our reality, it becomes obvious that they create perceptions. And perceptions change not only how you feel on doctor's visits as a kid, but also your self esteem, sense of personal worthiness, relationships, prosperity, a deserving mindset, job performance, physical and mental health, spiritual outlook and so on.

For instance, if you believe yourself to be a competent or incompetent person, a happy or unhappy woman, this changes your inner life completely, as well as the way you speak, act and show up in the world. It changes the way people see and treat your. It creates your outer life as a consequence too. It is a complete game-changer.

Do you know people of so-called average looks (those who don't seem at all special at first sight), but whose attitude, speech and ability to efficiently relate to others tell a very different story? A story of great self-esteem, for example. Conversely, you must have met highly attractive people, who are kind and wise, but whose low sense of worthiness makes them behave in a meek, self-deprecatory manner that makes them ultimately unattractive, and completely dilutes their power to bring their valuable inner self out into the world, in a way that could make an impact, in a way that influences others big time.

One great a-ha moment came for me when I realized that **state, or my feelings and thoughts in the present moment, are the stuff that life is made of.** That is what you have really, and that is what you are continuously after, feelings. Feelings of security, of excitement, of pride and fulfillment, of freedom, confidence, love, appreciation and joy. Think about it for a minute.

I have some bad news, and then some good news here: among the ten biggest regrets of dying people is not having lived more in a state of peace, calm, confidence and of enjoying one's daily life. Of spending too much time in states of regret, self-doubt, self-criticism, fearful anticipation, tension and rush.

As promised, there is one piece of amazingly good news, too. The best ever, if you ask me:

Since you are the one who generates your state, **you could always be in control of your thoughts and feelings. In control of the way you feel at any given moment, in control of steering your thoughts in the direction YOU desire.** You don't have to live like a fragile branch in the wind, merely reacting to events in your life, or following dreams that other people set for you.

You are not only able to create your emotional state; if you fully understand its importance, **you will make it a life mission to maintain your self in this wonderful state of enthusiastic, joyful confidence for the vast majority of the time.**

It is a skill anyone can learn. A habit anyone can practice. A muscle anyone can grow. I promise.

Chapter 5

WHAT DO YOU WANT?

---

*"Whatever things are true, whatever things are honest, whatever
things are just, whatever things are pure, whatever things
are lovely, whatever things are of good report; if there be any
virtue, and if there be any praise, think on these things."*

-Philippians 4.8 (The Bible, American King James Version)

We have explored together our essential life purpose, and we had a
glimpse of how our thoughts and emotions are the power engines that
build up (or down) our state in the present moment. We concluded
that state has a tremendous influence on our decisions, on the way
we approach reality - events and people in our life. And yes, decisions
(or lack thereof) influence the trajectory of our actions, and literally
steer our life in one direction or another.

So now you must be wondering, can we please talk about confidence
and how to always be in charge of your own life?

**Yes, yes, yes we are going to do it. So far we have been paving the
way for a better understanding of who you are, how you function
and what is the North point to never lose sight of. When we
understand why we do things, we tend to become more efficient.**

When we understand our own behavior and the thought-emotion process, we are no longer slaves to our mind, but rather the masters of it. While ignorance keep us stuck, clarity and understanding bring pure power to act wisely and consistently on a daily basis.

WHAT IS CONFIDENCE?

Confidence is a feeling of certainty: you think and feel that YOU CAN, that YOU WILL handle whatever comes your way, that you are the one who controls your life and your reality. Your thoughts and feelings shout "Yes!" with one voice, and your body experiences it and acts like you mean it. You are one strong machine, going forward full speed, all power horses pulling in the same direction.

State is a feeling. Feelings are our body's reaction to thoughts running through. Thoughts, the little voice inside our head, are the constant hidden dialogue we have with ourselves and the world. Emotions are our inherited or learnt responses, depending on what events mean to us. For example, if my childhood references include beliefs that fat old men dressed in red are dangerous for some reason, I will most probably have a lot of scared feelings during Christmas, therefore my usual (re) action will be to run away from Santa. And I'd miss all the fun and love and the spirit of Christmas.

A zoom into my mind and my emotions would display this process:
Thought: "Here's a fat old man dressed in red, he is dangerous" →
Emotion of fear →
State of defensiveness or aggressiveness, fight-or flight mode →
Decision to run →
Action: I run away!

This is a slow-motion picture of the process, in reality often it happens in seconds.

Now this is a caricature of an example, but imagine an enormous, red striped tiger in front of you, looking straight into your eyes, roaring, opening his huge mouth full of fangs and saying "Hello, dinner!". Now it would be really, really useful for you to have learned (and now think) that big, red animals are dangerous. That would save your life ☺

Do you see how some associations are in your favor, even healthy and life saving? While some others limit you and literally make you miss on your life, on developing your full potential and living your dreams.

Going all the way up, to the tip of the pyramid, we naturally wonder: **What are thoughts** and where do they come from?

Would you please pause for a moment and answer this:

Question: What is your next thought going to be?

I guess you cannot know.

I cannot.

Nobody can. That is because thoughts come from our subconscious mind and beyond, they are memories re-activated and replayed into our conscious minds. In this sense, our conscious minds are slaves of pre-programming and habit. Seriously. About 95% of our thoughts are just that, stories written by others, unconsciously replayed by us. Unless we learn how to change that and take control. How to access and tap into the type of thoughts that take us higher, forward.

So you cannot predict your next thought, because it comes from your subconscious mind.

What you CAN do is train your conscious mind – the final decision maker- to CHOOSE the positive, to choose a better direction: at any given moment you have the power to select a positive

interpretation of what is happening, to select the good in any person, thing or situation, so that the thoughts and feelings –your reaction - do not stray far beyond the realm of peace, balance, joy, acceptance, freedom and so on. We cannot fully control our incoming thoughts, but what we can control is our choice of WHICH THOUGHT TO FOCUS ON. That is why ancient philosophies and disciplines have been so keen on cultivating and training the power of focus, the power and discipline of the mind.

This is why I bring in front of you this crucial and extremely powerful commitment that you want to make here and now, for the rest of your life. It is a commitment I have made myself and it is the one most important decision I have ever made, a choice I keep making daily. If you want to be happy:

You now commit to love yourself so sincerely, every single day, that you will allow yourself to always follow Joy.

To love yourself enough to make it true in your heart that you have the birthright to be happy and free every single day of your life.

To never again give your power away by thinking otherwise, not even to blame and guilt yourself when you fall off the joy train! Because what blame and guilt do is they bring you back down into the gutter, far away from the feelings of lightness, freedom, confidence and appreciation that you just now committed to cultivate no matter what.

James Allen said it beautifully in "As a Man Thinketh": "Just as a gardener cultivates his plot, keeping it free from weeds, and growing the flowers and fruits which he requires, so may a man tend the garden of his mind, weeding out all the wrong, useless, and impure thoughts, and cultivating toward perfection the flowers and fruits of right, useful, and pure thoughts."

Focus on the good, on what feels constructive, empowering and free in any given moment.

BECOMING THE MASTER OF YOUR OWN LIFE

Mastering your inner dialogue is by far the most powerful thing you can do to master your emotional inner life. The way you speak to yourself can either break you down, or carry you far beyond the most impressive obstacles.

There are three main components that create your emotional canvass, the feeling of your life in any given moment. The great news is that you can change and control all three, they are all powerful and immediately available to you.

First is your physical body: your posture, your movements, your voice and your gestures, and so on. We all know a slacking posture, a low gaze and a whining voice perpetuate a feeling of discouragement, while standing tall, breathing regularly, talking loud and slowly immediately conjure a sense of confidence. Further, a healthy body fueled with great food and regular exercise gives you a far better feeling of strength and confidence than a weak, unhealthy one.

Second (but not less important) is the direction you give to your thoughts. The things that you focus on most of the time make up your reality, the strip of world you experience in the present moment. If you spend most of your day brooding over what you do not want, in regrets, worries, resentment and fear, your choices and actions will reflect it, and so will your life.

Conversely, if you concentrate on what you DO WANT, on what you like and what is going well, on constructive, positive outcomes and calculations, this will build up your confidence, and it will reflect in the way you see the world and act within it. Thoughts attract more similar thoughts. Things and experiences we focus on longer will attract more similar things and experiences. Confident people attract success and fulfillment. Remember, while you cannot control your next thought, you can always steer it in a better direction, you can rephrase and guide yourself with more empowering thoughts.

You may be currently wanting to lose weight and your running thoughts may sound like a poor, discouraging monologue: "how could I ever lose weight, since I never seem to carry through with any diet?". Here your brain – your loyal servant that needs to give you always some solutions - may have been practices into the habit of regularly answering, "because you are indolent and you have no discipline or will power".

What you can immediately do is re-phrase and set some more meaningful and empowering guidelines "My goal is to have great energy, strength and fitness, to feel good inside my body. I know others have done it, and I can do it too, all I need to do is keep going and praise myself more for my daily progress" Now that is a completely new perspective and your mind will come running to provide new answers: it may suggest that you take up more pleasant, less time-consuming activities, like dancing and high intensity interval training, that you do intermittent fasting instead of dieting, and so on.

Seek and you shall find!

I have become a master at optimizing my life and installing new and more empowering habits. I gave up smoking, become fitter and healthier than ever before, started waking up at five am to get in the best shape before I start my day. I trained my mind to do exactly what I am sharing with you (instead of running around in a downward spiral of negativity and despair). Most importantly I have been constantly learning how to love myself no matter what, and this has reflected in every single area of my life: my mind, my body, my relation with my Higher Guide, my relation with my children, my husband, my life purpose and my mission, my finances, my friendships, and so on.

The third important component to the way you feel is the story you constantly tell yourself in your head, and out loud to others, about the meaning of the world, events and people in your life. Have you noticed how you get a sudden feeling of respect, admiration, and attraction to people who are warm, kind, positive and supportive in their physiology and language? And you get equally repelled by constantly negative, whining or cynical individuals. At an energy level, there is a very solid explanation for that, it is about like attracting like and the Law of Attraction, but we will not delve into this here yet.

Now I am not asking you to pretend all is fine when it is not, and ignore reality completely. I do not mean that you should stop improving and just give yourself pep talks to see things through a rosy lens, no matter how bad they are.

While you are wisely analyzing your options, making decisions, setting out to take action, solve your problems and improve where necessary, you do so from a state of joy, confidence, and optimism, instead of one of fear, tension, anger or anxious anticipation. You approach all things with a clear strong vision of what you want them to be, of where you want them to go, and with a feeling of unshakeable certainty that it will be done.

This is the place of power and resourcefulness that you want to contemplate, think, speak and act from. You do not want to think, speak nor act from a place of fear. First you make yourself confident in your vision, and then everything else follows.

Therefore, I ask you to make another commitment today. I want you to print this page, cut off the part below, write the date, your name, SIGN IT and PUT IT IN A PLACE WHERE YOU CAN SEE IT FIFTY TIMES A DAY: on your mobile and computer desktop, make it a wallpaper; on your fridge, your desk, your mirror, inside your wallet, put a daily reminder in your phone about it.

Date:

I ……………………………………….now decide and resolve to make my inner state of peace, clarity, confidence and joy the number one priority of my life, regardless of circumstances.

I…………………………………………….understand that I am the only one in charge and responsible for the quality of my life, and that, as a Divine Creator, Life is here to support my every step. All I need to do is ask, and keep my heart high in gratitude, as it is already given.

I…………………………………..…………..now know with certainty that the quality of my life is given by the quality of my decisions, which are influenced by my inner state, my emotions and my beliefs.

I always follow joy, peace, clarity and confidence.

Signature:

Chapter 6

OBJECTIONS, YOUR HONOR!

A life of joy, peace, clarity and confidence. Every single day. Right.....

Seriously??

The first time I realized this is even possible, it felt like time stopped and everything was still. I was standing in the same place, and yet the magnitude of the realization left me in awe, magically transported in a new reality, a new world. The world was the same, but what had changed was my perception of it, and my awareness of the infinite possibilities suddenly opened in my face. It was like a wall of opaque glass had suddenly been shattered, and, while I could hear the pieces falling, I could also see the exhilarating light of day with clarity. Unmediated. Unobstructed.

Unlimited potential was now mine to have. Alice in wonderland could not have been more excited!

One of the biggest lies we learn (and then incorporate into our perception of the world) is that it is impossible to experience happiness every day, every hour, for however long and however strongly we choose to.

Happiness as in peace, confidence, curiosity, excitement, love, enthusiasm, joy, freedom, elation, adoration, balance, strength, connectedness, ease, trust, flow, clarity.

Happiness is a habit, a mindset, a skill. It can be practiced and learned, like riding the bicycle. Everything becomes possible when we get even a small glimpse of what our life could feel like, day in and day out; when we give ourselves permission to learn to be happy; when we realize that we, just as anyone else, deserve to be happy.

My outlook on life was very different before, so I completely understand if you have any objections, or find it hard to believe that you can experience daily happiness.

You may think that wanting to feel joyful and confident every single day is irresponsible. Selfish. Unrealistic. "How am I supposed to feel content and joyful most of the time?"

And so we often go on telling ourselves so many other "nice" things, so many lies that we have picked up from our family and from society. Things that ask us to lower our expectations from ourselves, and from what life can be, when all along we have been given and granted everything, we need only ask.

Let's take a look at the most common lies.

- "How can I even desire to be happy all the time, when others suffer so much? Isn't that selfish and self-centered?"

Dear friend, **it is <u>your</u> number one duty to be happy and healthy and put yourself as a first priority.**

It is not selfish, but wise: if you function well and are happy, you can be of assistance to others as well.

You know this advice: "Love your neighbor as you love yourself" and there is double wisdom in these words. **Give love, compassion and support to YOURSELF AND others. They didn't ask you to love yourself less than you love others, or to love others first.**

If you have children like I have, putting yourself last is a destructive example and a bad model, not to mention you will burn out soon. I know because I grew up watching my own mother doing it, and that has impacted my self image and expectations a lot, until I figured out what I was doing, why I was doing it, and what I wanted instead. Then it took me a while to actually give myself permission to go for what I wanted, but once I started, the Universe started sending all supportive elements my way, once more.

I am not saying it was my mother's fault – I actually have deep love and respect for her, since I have seen her pain and I cannot even begin to understand how she managed to pull through so many years of no happiness. She is one of the most amazing, strongest women I know.

I am saying that now we know there is a better way. That we want to display and role model self-esteem and a healthy personal image for our kids. That our happiness brings more to those around us, too, and it makes us more lovable and inspiring human beings.

Nobody is going to build you a statue or give you a medal for your self-neglect. Believe me, I have tried to get one for a long time☺

In fact, it is more likely that you will accumulate so much frustration, sadness and resentment that you will stand no chance of being a strong, energetic, clear-minded, supportive person in your family, your team or your community. You will soon hate your life, and pretty much everyone in it will seem to present only their faults and defects to you.

Go ahead then, full speed, and make sure you are happy: then and only then can you support and inspire others to do the same.

Tip: Happiness is contagious and confidence is attractive. So get on with it, my friend. No more apologies, no more dimming your light to adjust into limits and expectations you've allowed others to set for your life.

- "Religious scriptures and leaders speak to us about sins, and the need to suffer in order to make up for yours, and to be worthy of salvation. I need to accept that suffering is probably payment for my sins."

Religious scriptures were written and interpreted by people who, under the influence of their time and place, assigned a great importance to pain and punishment, in order to reinforce the will of the most powerful, or of the rulers. But at the core of all scriptures one truth unites them all: we are all worthy children of God, God lives within, and staying close to your joyful, loving divine essence will help you thrive, here and now. The core is not about mistakes and obedience and salvation after death, but about knowing where the true power lies: in the daily constant renewal of our union with our Creator.

In Romanian we use the expression "E pacat!" to say both "It's a sin" and "It's a pity." Certainly this is the real meaning of sin: a pity, an opportunity missed, out of ignorance, as we place ourselves mentally and emotionally in situations much lower than what we need to, if we want to live like Creators. It is a pity and it is a waste of life to stay low, to persist in sadness, anger and feelings of worthlessness, to speak and act from these states and the thoughts they inspire, while they are not the higher essence of who we truly are.

- "Being happy all the time is impossible. Happiness is a temporary state that comes and goes. You need to work hard for it, to earn it and deserve it."

Happiness is a habit, a muscle to be exercised, a virtue to be cultivated.

It is a God given right to all human beings, unconditionally.

It is your initial state when you come into this world. Babies are happy, naturally confident and their upset comes and goes like a quick summer storm. They restore their happiness in seconds, with no fear or resentment. They do not know negative self-talk, self-criticism.

They do not look at their little bodies and say "Yuck, look at those fat thighs and the rolls around my tummy!"

Their emotional resilience is amazing, they are so flexible in their view, so ready for change. They have a built-in GPS for happiness. We all do.

Only later do we learn to hold resentment, to live in fear, to criticize and despise ourselves and others.

Re-learning how to live joyfully on a daily basis, restoring your emotional wellbeing quickly, on your command, is a skill that can be learned. If I have learned it, then so can you.

Making certain <u>habits</u> a daily priority, your regular practice, ensures your base of stability, enthusiasm, energy, a positive outlook on your world and life.

It empowers you to summon and maintain a joyful state and a confident attitude.

I have an easy morning routine to put me in the right state for the day and I have embedded multiple habits throughout my day to help me run at best capacity: physically, emotionally, mentally, spiritually.

If you study the biographies of very healthy, confident, successful people, you will find out that, without exception, they have all built their balance and emotional resilience through daily habits.

What we want to remember is **to be very intentional about the state we want to choose, at all times. This requires us to:**

- **regularly pay attention to our thoughts and feelings and**
- **aim for the better ones.**

A disciple once asked his spiritual master, regarding emotional resilience: "Master, how come you never lose your balance?" And the wise man replied "I lose it more often that you do probably, but I regain it instantly."

Getting off the high-speed train of joy is natural and human, and it helps us continue to formulate what we want, our next direction for growth. But you just don't want to stay there too long.

This, of course, gets so much easier with practice. And since time will go by anyway, we might as well start practicing today ☺

- "There are so many conditions that must be met before I can even hope to be happy: I need to have complete safety and security, a perfect health, a perfect body; I need to have a loving and committed partner; I need that job; the children; the promotion; more time; more friends; less weight; less wrinkles; less work; less problems…..Aaaaaaaargh" You get the picture. There is no end to the reasons we could come up with, to delay our happiness. The issue here is that the more we practice the absence of joy, the less we are training ourselves in experiencing and expecting it, in feeling that it is normal. So when the job, partner and children come, we won't be able to stay happy anyway, because we never practiced it. Very soon we will start finding faults with the new status, too, and decide once more that happiness must be waiting at the next goalpost. Just like the horizon, it will keep moving.

We want to find reasons to be happy and content here and now, and make this our daily mission.

A young woman who was born without arms, Jessica Cox, never allowed this limitation to stand in the way of her dreams; she drives a car and flies a plane; she has a black belt in martial arts and surfs the waves on a surfboard. She plays piano and travels the world inspiring and motivating others to break free from their own (perceived) limitations. She understands more than many of us about artificial (perceived) limitations, happiness and living your true potential.

Think Andrea Bocelli, one of the best tenors of all time, who has been blind from the age of twelve, and yet his dreams were more powerful than his limitations.

Think Oprah Winfrey, abused as a child, turned out so successful and inspires millions.

The world is rich in such examples, we only need to look for them and use them as positive references, as reasons to believe that we, too, can achieve whatever it is we are after.

On the other hand, however, there are so many people who seem to have it all: health, love, success and money, and yet decide to systematically mess up their lives, or sadly, even end them.

So it is really not about our resources. It is about how resourceful we are, how creatively we use what we have, about our ability to see strengths and advantages in almost everything.

Why not simply choose to be happy and confident now, anyway, and then reach out for that dream job, dream partner, dream home, from a place of contentment, confidence, fully aware that it is a budding reality, starting to make its way to you, to materialize.

- "If I am confident and positive all the time, I will lose some of my friends. People do not like confident, happy people, they feel intimidated and insecure in their presence."

Wrong. People follow confident people and secretly want to be like them. Those who cannot do it are the ones you may lose, because you are a living proof that happiness is possible. And that forces them to either raise their standards and become like you, or try to dismantle your success and happiness in some way, to keep you down on the same level in their own mind.

You do have a choice: stay down there and keep a low profile forever, just to make them feel comfortable, or look and make place for other friends, who cherish your happy nature and success, who are grateful to be in your company, who want to learn and grow with you.

Stay close to people who want to see you flourish, who rejoice in your well-being.

- "My happiness is not under my control; it is not something I can create, but rather something that happens to me, kind of randomly, in such moments and conditions that are hard to replicate whenever I wish."

Your emotional state is your responsibility; do not wait for or expect anyone else to make you happy, you will be disappointed. Guaranteed. Nobody knows better than you what it is that you need. You alone must play detective and identify what makes you happy, by trying and experimenting with a variety of things. This is the fun of life. If you master your ability to make yourself happy, you are IT.

You are the only one who can choose what to focus on – the good or the "bad", the direction that you give to your thoughts, the reaction you have to the "outside" world and events. You always have a choice. And cultivating your state of joy and contentment is nobody else's duty but yours.

- "I have been studying happiness habits and cultivating a confident mindset for a while now, but I still find myself tripping, falling down in the unhappy gutter once in a while. I'm probably never going to really get it."

This is a forever-unfolding path. We are all constant work in progress, and the aim here is quick and easy bounce-back from the gutter, not flying high every single second. As long as we maintain the positive, constructive direction, as long as we stay on a path of growth, as long as we are committed to attend to our wellbeing and accept ourselves just as we are, where we are – we will bounce back in no time, and this is what mastery is all about.

Your staying in your unhappiness is always an available choice; but it will never make the world any better nor brighter, or help you progress in any way. It won't help anyone.

We invest so much of our time, thoughts and energy in things that do not serve us, but make us miserable or waste our life, around people who do not lift us any higher. **We could instead be making a routine for happiness our top priority**: the most astounding results will follow shortly.

Every morning you give so much time and attention to showering your body, brushing your teeth, putting on make up and the right clothes. Why would you leave something so important as your emotional state to chance? Why would you just hope that perhaps a few things would go your way today? Why not make sure, by tending to your mindset and emotions first, before you rush into the day?

As I said, confidence and emotional resilience are a muscle that we build. The purpose is to be able to summon the good emotions when you want them, and to be in control of your emotions and reactions to the world and events outside. To redirect your thoughts as often as necessary. When events or people trigger in you uncomfortable thoughts and feelings, you want to know how to give them an empowering meaning, one that allows you to feel better and inspires you to make the right decisions and go for the right actions.

When you meet with painful or uncomfortable situations, you want to have the understanding and practice required, in order to bounce back much faster, much easier, with the minimum amount of effort.

You want to be able to recognize the bright side at all times, so that you can never be lost again.

Chapter 7

YOUR UNAPOLOGETIC, CONFIDENT LIFE

God is a frequency that exists within you.
All you need to do is tune in.

-Unknown

You have just learned that it is possible to create a state of joy, peace and confidence at will, at any time in your day, every day.

You have previously grounded yourself in the understanding that you are part of a much larger scheme of things, that you are inherently supported (all you have to do is ask) and that the purpose of your life is to live your full potential, while enjoying and loving your every day.

This understanding, coupled with powerful strategies and habits, has the capacity to unleash your full potential. Fear is no longer going to hold you back from what you really want to achieve. You will finally be able to create your amazing life, and live it fully, every single day! All you need to do is take action consistently and build this knowledge and habits into your daily routines.

It is crucial that we define **which are the states that are desirable, in which we are most resourceful, and to learn quickly applicable techniques that can change our state in seconds (for the better).**

We have already spoken about how you want to feel most of the time: joyful, confident, peaceful, loving, free, creative, fun. You want to feel good, because this is the essence of Who you are.

You can use an emotion scale in any given moment, to identify where you are, and where you want to be heading.

Dr David Hawkins designed such a scale, and called it the Map of Consciousness, by building on the previous research of Drs George Goodheart and John Diamond, in the fields of applied and behavioral kinesiology. They discovered that our muscles become stronger or weaker in the presence of positive or negative stimuli (emotional, intellectual). In plain words, our muscles are more resistant to outside pressure when we contemplate something true or pleasant (when we have "good" emotions), while their strength decreases significantly when we say a lie, or think of something sad or unpleasant (experience a "negative" emotion).

In one of the most powerful books of all times, "Ask and It is Given", Esther and Jerry Hicks explain, through their conversations with Abraham that, as creators of our own life experience, we really only have one important question to ask ourselves: "How can I bring myself into vibrational alignment with my desires?" And the answer is by paying attention to the way we feel, to our emotions, and then deliberately choosing thoughts –about everything- that feel good to us when we think them.

The book also describes an Emotional Guidance Scale, that confirms the one devised by Dr Hawkins, and that lists emotions as follows, from the most pleasant and empowering, to the most uncomfortable and disruptive:

1. Joy/Appreciation/Empowered/ Freedom/Love
2. Passion
3. Enthusiasm/Eagerness/Happiness
4. Positive Expectation/Belief
5. Optimism
6. Hopefulness
7. Contentment
8. Boredom
9. Pessimism
10. Frustration/Irritation/Impatience
11. Overwhelment
12. Disappointment
13. Doubt
14. Worry
15. Blame
16. Discouragement
17. Anger
18. Revenge
19. Hatred/Rage
20. Jealousy
21. Insecurity/Guilt/Unworthiness
22. Fear/Grief/Depression/Despair/Powerlessness

In order to manifest our desires and intentions, we need to stay within the realm of the first seven categories, teaches Abraham. Simply put, we need to feel good, by contemplating thoughts or carrying actions that cultivate in us those emotions. When we feel anything less than that, our perception does not coincide with that of our inner Divine guidance, and we need to alter our perception to match it.

When we desire something, we need to feel the feeling of its already coming to reality. Hold this feeling, this image and these thoughts long enough, and it will materialize into our awareness, making it discoverable by our conscious senses. Conversely, if we focus on the lack of that which we desire, our subconscious and the universal forces at work will again collaborate to materialize what we are feeling: this time, a lack.

Do you remember being down and discouraged and how annoyed you felt when one of your friends told you to cheer up and think positive? The reason is that it makes us feel almost powerless: we know that thinking positively would make everything better, but we have no clue on **how to get there**, when we feel far away from anything positive right now?

Abraham teaches us to employ the Emotional Guidance Scale: the higher you are on the scale, the better you feel, and the easier it becomes to access more thoughts on the same level. Feel good, get creative ideas and solutions.

In order to intentionally use the Emotional Guidance Scale, we identify our current state of emotions, and we speak and think yourself up the scale, one emotion at a time. In other words, we contemplate thoughts that feel true and feel a little better to us, until we have reached a much better feeling place.

With practice at following Joy as North on your life compass, you can become so good at this that you can literally change your state in seconds. Remember that spiritual master who could regain inner balance almost instantly? You can do it too.

In less than a minute you have transformed the meaning of your experience, you have reached for empowering emotions and decided a new course of action. What a relief! **The key is to always reach for** the better and more empowering thought and the better feeling state, knowing that these bring you closer to what you want.

And why would you want to practice this?

Because of the commitment you made to yourself, to always aim for joy and to never again let yourself wallow in despair, guilt, shame or hopelessness.

It is plain and clear: our thoughts and emotions can empower or destroy us.

When you act from a state of fear, anger, guilt, confusion or shame, you are bound to act, think and make decisions that are not really in your best interest, for your highest good. You will not have confidence to think for yourself, you will only reach for far less than what you can really get, and you will be easily influenced by whoever happens to be around.

I am not telling you that you will have a life without challenges. What I am saying is that **you will be so emotionally fit that you will bounce back to contentment and confident optimism in little or no time, because you will have the emotional muscle, the know-how, the skills and practice to do so.**

OTHER TESTED AND VERY EFFICIENT RAPID STATE-ENHANCING STRATEGIES

I have personally tried all of these and use them on a daily basis. I guarantee that if you incorporate them in your daily practice, you will soon use them automatically, like a master☺ Take the list, print it and keep it nearby where you can see it. Put reminders on your phone, computer, mirror, etc. Make them simple habits and you will notice tremendous changes in the way you feel, think and act. I guarantee it.

1. CALL FOR HELP

As in Divine Help.

Call for Jesus, Krishna, Buddha, the Archangel Michael, the Higher Power, God, or the name that you assign to God or Divine Intelligence. With strong belief and desire, ask that it lifts your heart and mind from sadness and into comfort, freedom, love, confidence and light. You can do this any time, anywhere.

It never failed me once. Not once.

An old advice says, "Pray before you think", and it is a very wise and logical advice. When you know that your mind is a receiver, much more than it is an emitter; when you know that a certain kind of thought, maintained long enough, attracts more thoughts like it – you want to remind yourself often to set your receiving frequency on a good and constructive one. Calling Love and Clarity to uplift, inspire and guide you is always a good idea, before thinking, during thinking, after thinking.

2. USE YOUR BODY DIFFERENTLY

Using your body to change your mood may seem superficial and "mechanic", but it is nothing but. Your body is a power machine, and knowing how to employ its resources wisely is golden. Your postures, your tone of voice, your breathing patterns, the speed of your movements (or lack thereof), they can all give you a fast track to happiness and confidence, or on the contrary, to sadness and discouragement.

Just like the principle "Fake it till you become it", your body changes trigger signals to your mind that you are ready to enter a different state, and so the mind will soon play along and hop on the happy train.

What **quick magic your BODY can do for your MOOD:**
- **Take several deep breaths**: inhale on count to 4, hold for 12, exhale for 8 (4-12-8).

- **Alternate nostril breathing** is a brilliant and simple breathing exercise that only takes a minute of your time, but has tremendous benefits, such as the newly increased levels of oxygen in your blood and brain, that immediately reduce anxiety and stress (and push you up that emotion scale!). Use the thumb and little finger of your right hand. Keep your mouth closed at all times. The thumb completely closes your right nostril, while you inhale with the left. Hold for a few seconds, release your thumb, close the left nostril with your little finger, and exhale through your right nostril. Inhale through the right nostril now, while you keep your little finger in place on the left. Hold, release, close the right nostril again with your thumb, and exhale. Repeat five to ten times.

- **Smile!** Studies prove that within seconds your mood is bound to improve! Put on a big wide smile and your brain will soon take you seriously.

- **Stand tall and adopt "Power Postures",** poses of confidence that influence testosterone and cortisol levels in the brain, make your mind believe that you are confident, and give you much better chances for success. Amy Cuddy's brilliant TED Talk demonstrates the poses in detail.

- **Speak loud and clear, in a calm and gradually more enthusiastic tone:** the tone and speed of your speech can alter your mood in seconds too. (Conversely, watch out for your mood changing when you "whine" about something long enough, or when you speak in an angry tone. As Tony Robbins says, people do not get depression, they DO depression. Not in one day, it is true, but going down and down over a period of time. With the exception of tragic events, it usually takes serious and constant habits to end up in depression).

- **Explosive movements** on your favorite upbeat music- I bet you remember those party times when you felt on top of the world dancing and singing with your friends! Take those experiences and include them in your daily morning routine. Make the best playlist you can and keep it close. I have different playlists in my smartphone and YouTube to instantly put me in the chosen mood and state. Listening to them repeatedly, I have associated best feelings and thoughts to them, so when I need a boost, this one works magic too.

4. FOCUS ON CONSTRUCTIVE, GOOD FEELING THOUGHTS, AND CHANGE YOUR INNER DIALOGUE

- **Shout out your favorite incantations:** take affirmations such as "I'm happy, strong, prosperous and loved!" and shout them out with feeling, as if you fully believe them! (No, this is not a funny story, but seriously documented research, applied and tested over and over again by myself and the best coaches, athletes and successful people of the moment).

- **Closely monitor your thoughts and choose the ones that feel better.** As we agreed, this is not about ignoring reality, but about choosing emotions and thoughts that empower you to take constructive action. The more you practice observing your feelings and your thoughts, the better and faster you will get at steering away from disempowering ones.

- **When you seem to hit a wall, a dead end situation again and again, remind yourself that it is only a matter of perception and ask yourself better questions** Instead of asking yourself "Why can't I ever get into my fittest shape?" (dead-end, hit-a-wall kind of question), rephrase it into a smarter "What would it take for me to become a strong and healthy size eight, easily and effortlessly, and to have fun in the process?" Your mind will start finding the solutions, just ask it the proper questions and give it clear requests. In this case, it may suggest that you can go dancing and canoeing, do weight-lifting instead of cardio, go for intermittent fasting instead of the latest fad diet, have a standing desk instead of sitting while you work, and so on.

- **Focus on what is going on well and FEEL the feeling of gratitude for these things.** I mean really feel it, not just mumble it. It could be your health, your kids, your education, your home, the weather, a flower, the sunrise, a song, some newfound clarity or awareness, anything can make a good reason to be grateful, find at least five and write them down. I do every morning, and many times throughout the day I remind myself to focus on what I like in my experience; with practice, it literally becomes your second nature.

But there is no better time than the present. Let us take two minutes, here and now, to list fifteen things that you enjoy: ideas, people, feelings, qualities, aspects, anything that comes to mind that you appreciate. You may already have this ability, but it is still worth writing about your reasons of appreciation, to experience the instant magic.

Things, people, ideas, aspects I like, appreciate, feel grateful for:
1.
2.
3.
4.
5.
6.
7.
8.
9.
10.
11.
12.
13.
14.
15.

Here are some of the things that I appreciate, right here and now, to share an example of gratitude avalanche: my health, my loved ones-family and friends, my connection with God, my clarity, amazing role models and mentors, fantastic students, the round table I am seated at while writing now, my laptop, my mobile phone, the lovely coffee barista's smile and her friendly presence, the shimmering sun light on the sea, my ability to see, breathing freely, my comfortable light cotton dress, trees and flags and umbrellas fluttering in the wind outside, my childhood, my grandparents' village, access to every technology and opportunity, the fact that we are alive in the most amazing times humanity has ever seen, where life is good and rich with endless possibilities for exponential growth...

You may have noticed that your emotional state and the way you perceive reality has transformed completely, before you even reached fifteen!

- **Focus on WHAT YOU WANT**, not on what you hate/dislike/ resent. So many of us invest all their energy into fearful and resentful thoughts that never get them anywhere. Instead you want to:

1. Formulate your desired outcome clearly for this situation and see it happening: the excitement and anticipation generated by your actually seeing it happen will help keep you motivated to act.

2. Brainstorm a series of actions you can take to reach this outcome. Assess what it would take to make it happen: people, resources, etc. and feel for the most inspired course or path ahead. Ask for Guidance in meditation, prayer and free writing.

3. Take action in this direction and keep your thoughts focused on WHAT YOU WANT, on any other thoughts that make you feel good. Whenever you find yourself straying, re-direct your thoughts, again and again, as many times as it takes.

Let us take one goal that you have had trouble achieving and rephrase it in a meaningful and empowering way:

YOUR INITIAL GOAL

....

A BETTER QUESTION:
What would it take for me to

....

My example:

Goal: To wake up at 5.30 am.

I used to find it difficult to wake up at 5.30 a.m., to give myself the time to prepare and greet the day at my best.

After several failures, my initial thoughts were of frustration, such as "Why can't I ever wake up on time?"

Soon I found better questions for myself:

- "What would it take for me to be able to wake up at 5am daily motivated and eager to start the day?" "What kind of things would be so important and pleasant that I will be eager to wake up?"
- "Why do I want to wake up at 5.30 am?" To give myself time to prepare for the day and be my best version.
- "What will I gain?" ME time: starting the day connected to my Creator, choosing my intentions for the day, silence, prayer, thinking grateful thoughts and asking for what I need. Planning my actions for the Day and blessing my loved ones. Time to take care of my body (exercise, breathe, take shower etc.), my mind (do my short powerful meditations), my emotions, and my spirit. Starting the day grounded, supported, peaceful, happy, confident, protected, focused, knowing exactly who I am and who I am going to be today.
- "What happens if I keep failing to do this?" The day finds me unprepared. I am more likely to react to events, instead of acting in a way that is consistent with who I want to be (e.g. I am more likely to lose focus and not follow on things I want to do; I am more likely to get tensed; overwhelmed; nervous; this is not who I want to be)

- "What are the things that will help me wake up and keep my promise to myself?" Sleep at a decent hour, latest by 10-10.30, no matter what. Put a pleasant alarm song on my mobile phone. Determine and commit that I will get out of bed at the first alarm. Have my two liters of water ready to warm up by the stove, and the coffee nearby.

Chapter 8

THE HIDDEN "ENEMIES"

You have now learned how to use the Emotional Guidance Scale to move from disempowering emotional states and thoughts, to constructive and empowering ones, within seconds.

You understand that your body is a powerful wizard that can magically improve your mood instantly, by addressing your posture, your breathing, your voice and so on. "Fake it till you become it" is a very valuable tool in this sense too: you start behaving like a happy confident person and you soon feel like one. Just to confirm, these are solutions based on serious studies, done by professional researchers with tens of thousands of people, and confirmed by numerous successful men and women.

In other chapters you will begin to learn about how to powerfully design your masterpiece life. You will learn to unleash the power of great goals, aligned with your values, to create balance, power and forward momentum in all areas of your life.

But before we go there, there are two very hot things we need to handle. Two things that could obstruct all that, all your growth and development in you health; your relationships; your finances; self-love and personal evolution.

Imagine designing your dream life, but never actually getting there. Your dreams remaining constantly far on the horizon, never materializing. Such a desolate perspective of loss, and it applies to so many people out there. Many of us never even realize where is the saboteur, and settle for the bitter feeling that "probably this is all there is to life".

The number one saboteur is right inside our minds, and it is called limiting beliefs.

A limiting belief is nothing but a view that you hold with certainty, something you have strong feelings about, but which actually disempowers you in so many ways. It may be something you are aware of, or something so subtle that you never consciously think about it.

A classical one with women especially revolves around **deserving**: we often deny ourselves progress, good care and good health, or reaching for our dreams, because somewhere along the way we came to believe that we are not worthy. Not deserving of a good life. Not deserving joy and the fulfillment of our deepest desires.

Some limiting beliefs can be as obvious as "I am a mother, I must sacrifice everything for the wellbeing of my family." (You are a person too, remember, born to live in joy and to fulfill your potential) How many of us have grown up seeing our mothers neglecting themselves, physically and emotionally, denying themselves their dreams and desires, sometimes even the smallest joys of life, just because that is what they believed they should do – in order to stay true to, and congruent with their personal images of what a good mother should be. Yet how much sorrow and frustration they were actually experiencing!

How many of these expectations and limitations even belong to you, and how many come embedded into your subconscious from an early age, learned from family, teachers and other role models? And then we take them for reality, they layer deep inside our minds and we never come to question them again. They become laws we never even question, so profoundly intertwined in our identity that we don't even realize they are there anymore.

Make it a habit to be a bit suspicious of your negative, cynical or destructive thoughts, since we learned that thoughts come from the subconscious mind.

They are learned "programs" if you wish, and THEY ARE NOT YOU. Yes, your mind is not You, the vast majority of your thoughts are stories from the subconscious, chain reactions replayed incessantly by the record player that is our mind.

Make it a habit to stop yourself often and watch them. Ask yourself whose values and beliefs are these? How do they serve you? Do they help you grow, or do they keep you nailed down, revolving in the same maddening circles of repeated failure?

Ask yourself questions like:
- **Why should I do this?**
- **Whose expectations am I trying to fulfill here: do I want them to be my own standards?**
- **When did I learn that I have to be this way, in order to deserve and to be worthy?**
- **What is it that I actually want here? What is my desired outcome from this situation?**

These are very powerful questions. You do remember that we spoke about always **shifting your attention, your thoughts and focus on that which you want** (not on the unwanted). Here is the part where you make sure that this is really what **you** want, and not somebody else's dreams, standards and values.

Some limiting beliefs are much more subtle.

For example, after a good amount of introspection (and of halting and questioning my own thoughts), I realized the reason why I wasn't able to reach my optimum weight and look and behave my best, confidently. It wasn't lack of discipline, or lack of a plan. I found that I had some underlying belief that good looking, confident women are often perceived as threats by their girl friends and female colleagues. And since my core identity was being a nice, loving, supportive girl, I wouldn't let myself shine, for fear it would turn away my friends. The problem was that the belief was so subtle and so deeply buried, it was like background traffic noise, if you wish, sounds that you get used to so much that you forget they are there at all. I had never expressed this fear or thought about it clearly, in words before, so finding this belief, facing it and replacing it with a more empowering one was a life changer for me.

Also, another conviction was that I had to "make it", to achieve success through my wits, my intelligence, my skills, my education and my talents; including good looks in this equation was almost vulgar, unconceivable. This belief had some connection to dialogues I had heard during my whole young life, where successful women were catalogued as "easy" and suspected of using their beauty charms to climb the social ladder and advance in their careers.

You can see how much these references can influence our lives, our success or lack thereof, in any one of our areas of interest: health, abundance, love, career, spirituality, networking and so on.

We don't just pick up other people's stories. We create some ourselves, when we formulate generalizations and conclusions that simply do not serve us. They may be true for some people, but they do not have to be true for all.

A classic example is the person who had a cheating partner, and comes to believe that all future partners will eventually cheat. Guess what that will do? Even if you find the most amazing, loving partner, your expectation that he or she will eventually cheat will make you speak and behave in certain ways that may eventually bring your worst fears to reality. You will sooner or later become cynical, disengaged, commanding, bitter, cold and so on, just because you assume that he or she will behave in the same way like your previous partner. You will make your worst fears come true, again and again.

How do you, then, spot limiting beliefs, and how do you release them and replace them with empowering ones?

If you remember, our mind actually has a mind of its own in a way: we have a conscious and a subconscious mind that have different functions; the first is about will power, the second is habitual; they also have very different processing powers (2000 bits/second versus 4 billion bits/second of the subconscious.) They also receive and process information differently.

Therefore, if you keep addressing the subconscious with tools and means that only reach the conscious, you can end up stuck there for months and years, or sometimes forever. Do you remember how many times you consciously resolved and motivated yourself to quit smoking? Lose weight? Stop shouting at your children? To only find yourself off track again the very next day.

That is because the news of your resolution has not reached the subconscious, your storage of values, beliefs and attitudes that support and create consistent action and behavior. Your conscious says "But I have decided to stop smoking!" and the next time you reach for the cigarette and fill up your lungs with smoke, that was your subconscious saying "Nope, I haven't decided anything. I am not convinced." Experts call this cross-purposes or cross-references, meaning the two minds operating on conflicting premises.

Understanding this distinction now, we face the two categories differently.

1. **CONSCIOUS beliefs** Here it is pretty clear: on any given problematic area of your life you can think and list any limiting belief you can come up with. You can address them with the Emotional Freedom Technique or the ancient Hawaiian problem solving technique, Ho'oponopono. Both access your being from levels beyond the mere "physical", and they both yield results very fast.

EFT incorporates traditional Chinese medicine principles and approaches problems, emotions and solutions via energy meridians that further work it through your mind and body.

Ho'oponopono also grounds you into a much larger reality, and sends the right energetic messages to the Divine, the Universe and yourself, messages that clear, correct and resolve problems.

2. **SUBCONSCIOUS beliefs** The tricky part with these ones is that you are not consciously aware of them, right?

The way to reach your subconscious fast (yes, thank God there is a way) and bring out these beliefs into your conscious mind is by muscle testing. A beautiful bio-feedback mechanism similar to a lie-detector, integrated in our bodies, employed and documented in methods such as **Psych K (for beliefs)** and **The Emotions Code (for trapped emotions).**

The **muscle testing method** is widely used nowadays by many coaches, health practitioners, therapists and not only. How it works: since our subconscious minds control our physiological processes, a true statement would generate a higher resistance in our muscles; conversely, a false affirmation results in lower resistance, because it conflicts with the truth (that our subconscious knows- it stores everything, really) and short-circuits the electrical signals the carry commands from our brain to our muscles.

In case if you are wondering, these are thoroughly tested and proven methods, employed successfully by myself and thousands of others. They are very powerful, work very fast and do not require any resources or sophisticated knowledge. Go look them up, learn the methods, look for a practitioner to help you at first if you wish.

One other very simple thing to do is **free writing or journaling**. You could do it right now. When you are alone and writing freely, without focusing on a certain objective, but just allowing things to surface, information tends to ascend from your subconscious and into your conscious mind much faster. Hang in there for ten to fifteen minutes and keep writing, you will be amazed and relieved to see things so clearly. You have so much to gain, so many obstacles will be removed, that used to keep you stuck, blocked and unable to act.

There was a time when I was stuck in creating a successful product. I would procrastinate; delay; find all sorts of excuses not to act in a consistent and massive way to finalize this dream of mine.

While meditating and free writing, it surfaced that I actually associated this product with my financial independence, and that would mean total freedom to live life on my terms and possibly end my marriage that was in a delicate place at the time. Further deep, I had many references and conclusions dwelling in my subconscious mind (subtle, unspoken but there so strong) that financially independent women rarely have a happy family life; that they end up valuing their work more than their children and partner; that they can hardly ever find a partner who can tolerate their success and independence; that they ultimately end up so engulfed in dreams of success and career that they inevitably lose family and love. And family and love had always been my deepest, dearest values. What a revelation.

From here I worked backwards up, taking each identified belief and negotiating with myself, proving that it is not at all real, not for me, because I really know who I am. Giving myself strong arguments and solutions. The same day I started working like never before, because I now knew my dream wouldn't cost me my character, my time with my children, my ability to be lovable and loved.

Now is as good a time as ever to take those ten minutes to explore the two powerful exercises below, and please remember that you are in a process. Keep practicing, have patience with yourself and results will show soon. If you want a different life, you need to start doing different things. Your knowledge is becoming useful when you actually apply it.

Power Homework Part One

Take a look at the list below; these are some of the most common beliefs that hold the majority of people back at any given moment. They deeply resonate with most of my clients, when they come to see me.

This is just to get you started and give you a better idea of what you are looking for. For the fun of it, go through the list and give a percentage number to each belief (from 0 to 100), to reflect how true this feels for you.

As you go through them, you will probably start receiving more insight into other disempowering beliefs that you hold.

I don't deserve to be happy.
I don't deserve to be loved.
I don't deserve to be wealthy and abundant.
I cannot change.
I am a failure and there is no hope for me.
I have made mistakes and I deserve to suffer.
I am not in control of my life.
I will be happy when I get the perfect body. The perfect partner. Enough money to feel safe. The dream house. The kids. The job. And so on.
I need to sacrifice my happiness for my loved ones.
I am never going to be as good as others.
I am guilty.
I am worthless and incapable.
I am powerless.

Power Homework Part Two

Take one area of your life that you have tried to improve for a long time and have not succeeded yet (in a meaningful way). Start writing about it, list all related limiting beliefs that you are aware of, and let your hand take over, let your mind speak to you whatever comes out. You will have amazing surprises. It is just you and the paper, you don't even need to share it with me. Do it now, please, you will thank yourself later.

Chapter 9

FEARS

"You don't have to feel like a waste of space;
You're original, cannot be replaced.
If you only knew what the future holds,
After a hurricane comes a rainbow.
Maybe the reason why all the doors are closed:
So you could open one that leads you to the perfect road!"

-Katy Perry - Fireworks

You have now learned about your internal saboteurs, the limiting beliefs that we all absorb from parents and society, or construct ourselves based on our life experiences.

You have learned to always question the reasons why you find yourself apparently stuck in different areas of your life. Now you have several powerful and tested tools to employ every time you feel blocked.

Now we have reached the point where we can blast our way through one very common obstacle in the way of our building a happy confident life: our fears.

I used to live with them day and night, from the time I woke up until I went to sleep at night. I used to fear almost everything, worry about things large and small (most never came to happen), and as a consequence I passed numerous opportunities, abandoned brilliant ideas and avoided wonderful people because of my fears and my low self esteem (translated as "fear of failure and rejection").

There is a simple, healthy type of fear that is a natural reaction of self-defense, the fight-or-flight instinct that is supposed to kick in our adrenaline rush and help us survive in physically challenging situations. Such as running into a wild animal in the forest. That instant panic reaction is meant to mobilize all your physical energy for survival.

Nowadays though, we are rarely confronted with such clear-cut survival issues, or tigers in the wilderness. And yet we have learned fearful responses to other perceived threats: our boss, deadlines, our children screaming, terrorist attacks and crime in the news. They call it *stress*, but stress is nothing else but a constant state of fear, because we do not actually know how to deal with a certain perceived threat or another. We are not sure that we will be able to deal with it successfully, and so the fears remains there, unresolved, a buzzing constant background noise in our lives.

On your scale of human emotions, fear is a very low vibration energy, a very disempowering one. The more you stay in fear, the farther you are from your self-confident, joyful, powerful state. Make it your aim and your goal to become a master at conquering, at re-framing your fears, in a way that allows you to feel empowered, hopeful, supported.

Every single human being experiences fear in a variety of situations. What the successful, confident, strong people do differently is the way they deal with their fears.

Instead of allowing fear to freeze us, we always have the choice of grounding ourselves in something much higher, a power far greater than us, and see the good, the positive and the solutions in every situation, to get us in an empowered state where we will set ourselves in motion and take constructive action.

Look around you at any given moment and you will see tens and hundreds of people who, just like you, walk with a poker face, sometimes with a smile, but most of them with fear in their hearts. Do not let fear paralyze you. Do not let it rob you of your dreams. Do not let it stop you from doing what you know deep inside your heart is the best thing for you.

The greatest fear of my life was always losing my loved ones. For many years, nothing and no one could scare me more.

As a young girl I remember making silly, innocent calculations, estimating who was the oldest and who would go first. I would estimate that my grandparents would pass first, and then everybody else. Of course this is not how it works in reality, each of us choose our own time.

This most amazing and loving woman I knew, a family member, had been very ill for a long time. That morning when her son called me, I knew the fear in his voice meant she was not well at all.

But it was worse than I expected. Two hours later she was hallucinating in excruciating pains and soon fell into a deep coma. There was a sheer sense of horror, of terror, of deep fear in the home. In my heart. I was watching a loved one dying in great pain, and all her loved ones feeling powerless, hopeless and emotionally drained after they had been by her side through her battles for years.

When the ambulance came, I rode with her and her husband. When the doctors received her, I was the only one who had enough energy left to go in and stay with her. Every single cell in me and every nerve were screaming "Run!" The most paralyzing fear had taken over me. But I knew I could never face myself if I ran and left her to die alone in that hospital bed. I didn't know what to do, because apparently there was nothing that could be done.

Except let love take over.

I looked at her dear face, held her hand and said a heartfelt prayer for her and her relief, through my tears. Few minutes later she was gone.

I know you must have lost loved ones, too. The only reason I am sharing this with you is not to startle you, or make you sad, but to show that the only thing more powerful than fear is love. Love pushed me through so many incredible blocks, my strong belief in something immortal and far more precious and greater than my fear in the moment. Something I had to make a stand for, right then and there, for her and for myself, too.

We are not our fears. We are not our worries, anger or resentment, they are just the temporary color of our perception in the moment. We, in essence, are infinite, everlasting love and vibrant freedom, and that does not change because of temporary fear. The love core remains unchanged, regardless of our thoughts and life experience. When this distinction sinks in, we understand and perceive ourselves on two layers: the peaceful observer and the one who feels and experiences life through the senses and the lens of our beliefs and associations. We can always take a step back into observer mode. Into love.

This wonderful woman was fifty when she died. She had spent the last ten years of her life battling illness, having repeated surgeries and gruesome treatments.

I have two choices: to see her life through eyes of fear, or to see her life through eyes of love. To see her as the woman who died of a terrible illness. Or to celebrate the woman who was an inspiration for so many, always laughing and fun. To love life deeply and go for my dreams: she wanted to travel the world and took on a side job as a travel guide, despite the fact that loved ones did not quite support it. Imagine her regrets if she had not done it!!

My choice is clear: I am planning to honor her memory by living a long, healthy, happy, amazing life.

I can also choose to learn other lessons from her life: to ask for help and support and accept it; to take great care of myself and do anything it takes to restore my good feelings and my vibrant health, to love myself dearly and to gather supportive, uplifting people around me.

In any given moment, we have a conscious, intentional choice to make: to aim for love's perspective, or to give into anything less. To perceive from anything less. I am not saying it is easy at the start. It was not easy in the beginning for me, either. All I am saying is that it does get easier with practice, and this is a continuous process that does, at a certain point, take us over. The good wave takes us over, and becomes the dominant basis from which we experience our lives, by default, without having to try no more.

The benefits? Infinite. Love instead of fear provides solid confidence, as you rely on the endless resources and strength of the Divine within. Better health, better relations, more prosperity and abundance. And the best of all, for me, is an ability to live daily life with a feeling of enchantment. Of experiencing magic at every step.

This is no simple conversation, it is pure science. The way we choose to see things and experiences, the meaning we give to events in our heads, will make the difference between a life lived in dread, waiting for disaster and disease to strike, or a life of vibrant energy, health, happiness and constant progress. The difference is so tremendous, like choosing between life in black and grey, versus life in effervescent color. Choose well, choose now, it really matters.

Choosing good-feeling thoughts and empowering perspectives is the best skill one can learn.

Training yourself into this skill is done by repeatedly choosing better feeling thoughts, again and again, until it becomes our default response to life. And it will.

A very helpful tool in following your chosen, better-feeling direction is to have frequent, omnipresent reminders and incentives about your decision.

Amazing incantations, such as the ones offered by Louise Hay or Anthony Robbins in their books and courses helped me literally re-shape my neuro circuitry, build in new reactions and response mechanisms, as well as almost instantly release all fears.

Make one of your own, print it and stick it onto your mirror, display it on your mobile phone, your Pinterest boards, in your brain and your heart. Teach it to your children and your friends. Soak your mind and your environment with good reminders, and take a few moments as often as you can to think about what they mean. Not just to read them mechanically, but to think and feel what you would think and feel if you really believed those affirmations.

Affirmations work best when you repeat them in a state of emotional excitement, accompanied by explosive body movements, so that they become incantations. When you associate yourself with what you are saying, when you believe what you are saying, you prove your congruence through strong emotions, and your subconscious takes you seriously and accepts the new program or belief. It obeys your command. The new thought becomes the new reality, as you find a way to talk yourself into believing what you want, by contemplating things you already believe to be true and by putting yourself in the most vibrant, powerful positive emotional states.

If you have been doing affirmations with no results, this is the reason: your emotional state did not match your request. Now you know, so go get excited (not just a little bit hyped, but crazy like a locomotive) and start all over!

Chapter 10

MORE FEARS

We now have a clear distinction between the two type of fears: a natural reaction meant to help you survive or withdraw from danger, versus the energy-sapping background feeling of worry, doubt and mistrust in your own capacity to deal with things as they arise.

All wise and successful men and women ground themselves in a strong connection with a benign and loving higher power, that helps them navigate times when their personal resources have reached the limit and everything seems out of control. A power that provides an empowering meaning to situations that would otherwise seem tragic or unjust.

You now have a very efficient incantation to use in your daily life and I am sure that you have already learned it by heart and you are reciting it with great enthusiasm, at least twenty times a day. Right?

Today I would like to share a few other very powerful ways to deal with fear as it arises, because we need immediately applicable solutions don't we? We don't want to wait until it grows bigger than what we can handle.

There are times when rationalizing and solving the problems in your head just won't work, because oftentimes some feelings just won't leave. Remember, fear is a feeling triggered by a thought running through your body, a chemical reaction triggered by your nervous system, a certain type of electromagnetic energy. Seeing it from various angles allows you to understand how and why it can be approached in multiple manners.

The need for such solutions has kept me researching, testing, experimenting for over twenty years, and these are some of my favorites.

Please give yourself patience and love while you experiment with any and all of them over the next days and weeks. See what works best for you, and enjoy yourself in the process. Reminder: These are powerful, tested methods that do work and do have instant results.

1. **Prayer.** Fastest solution. Call upon your favorite higher power or the archangels to help release your fears. Archangel Michael is one of my favorite protectors and I have countless stories to tell you about the protection me and my loved ones have received instantly from him.
   One morning, we were driving on a six-lane highway in Dubai, with tens and hundreds of cars traveling at speeds over hundred kilometers per hour. I had an instant feeling of dread and fear, and remembered to call upon archangel Michael for protection (I usually do it also as part of my every morning routine, but you can call for help at any given time, these amazing guardians are on call 24/7). I didn't say a word, but I watched my husband, who was driving the car, change the lane with no apparent reason. Only five seconds later two cars collided in the place where we should have been. We were both shocked and my instant reaction was to ask in my mind, "Was it you, Michael? Give me a sign!" As

I looked to my side of the road, a huge blue sign read "Chez Michel". At Michael's.

This is a true story. My husband had no logical explanation for why he had changed the lane, it was "one of those impulse things". And this is just one out of countless such events I can share.

2. At any time and in any place you can **reconnect energetically with our Source to clear your energy and raise your vibration**: visualize and aim your consciousness about a hundred meters high, connect to the light (imagining it is enough to do the trick), feel or see the light flowing into your crown, your head, filling up your neck, chest, abdomen, pelvis, arms and legs and shooting down straight into the center of the Earth. From there it returns, refilling your body one more time. Focus this incoming light into your heart with a powerful intention to clear your fear. Visualize or feel this light for as long as you need, a few seconds or a few minutes. It always works.

3. **Emotional Freedom Technique**: tapping along certain pressopuncture point is very efficient at interrupting the flow of fight-or-flight response chemicals in your brain and gives you relief within minutes.

4. **Instant release of persisting or recent negative emotions, using the Emotions Code technique.** An extremely powerful and efficient tool.

   If you wish to learn more about EFT and the Emotion Code, you can always read The Tapping Solution by Nick Ortner, and The Emotions Code by Dr Bradley Nelson.

5. **Free writing**: this is another tool that helps you gain full understanding of your fear, assess all possible outcome

scenarios and brainstorm solutions to the perceived problems. Most worries dissipate in the light of understanding.

6. **Changing your emotional state**: remember we have learned how to do this by changing our:
   a. Internal dialogue, to a more positive and empowering one.
   b. Our body physiology: start moving, dancing, deep breathing 4-12-8, take on a Power Posture, speak calmer, smile (fake it till you make it)
   c. Find the paralyzing meaning you give your "problem", and look for a more empowering angle, a more constructive approach.

7. Last but not least, **reconsider this feeling not as paralyzing fear, but as a powerful impulse to get excited and ready for action**. Turn the black glove of fear inside out, into a bright yellow of eagerness and high-pitch excitement!

I strongly encourage you to take the time over the coming days, weeks and months to practice and experiment with all these methods. Make them part of your routine. Play and explore, read more, ask yourself questions and above all, **write every day about your insights and progress. Keeping track of my findings, revelations and results has been one of my most valuable habits.**

Most of these practices are as old as humanity. I have tried them with tremendous success, and I have seen other successful people employing them in their daily experience. All are thoroughly tested and proven to work again and again.

The key here, of course, is practice. As in "YOU are now starting to practice" ☺

You now have the knowledge and the tools; it is time for consistent daily action. Keep in mind that you have taken full responsibility for creating powerful changes in your patterns, so that you can create new habits and new reactions, to get back on track fast, and never feel hopeless again.

This is a journey in which you need to give yourself the time and the patience to grow at your own pace and, most of all, to love and accept yourself in the process.

Depending on how strongly you feel about changing, I know that you will make more time to learn and grow.

Just one word of caution, please, do not wait until all areas of your life are out of balance before you learn and take action. Learn before you need to.

Chapter 11

YOUR LIFE COMPASS
DIRECTION: VALUES

TIME FOR UNAPOLOGETIC, CONFIDENT DESIGN. YOU, DESIGNING YOUR LIFE LIKE A BOSS, JUST THE WAY YOU WANT IT

You now understand who you are, why you are here and what is the main purpose of your existence: experiencing the joy of creation, and constantly growing into your permanently expanding potential.

You have your compass pointing to the North of joy and freedom, and you are now aware that you are the only person responsible for, and capable of making you experience daily happiness.

We recognize limiting beliefs and fears, and know how to how to deal with them fast and effectively, so that we never become hopeless again. With practice, you know you will experience tremendous changes for the better, until one good day confidence becomes your dominant state of life.

The second part of this book aims to assist you in designing and building your life, on your own terms. This is about the new you, the one equipped with the knowledge and tools to become who you were really meant to be.

The vast majority of us spend our life wandering, picking up apparently random values and guidance and targets as they come, from our parents, teachers, friends and society. Based on that, most of us build up preferences, likes or dislikes, decision-making patterns. We classify things between good and bad, healthy and unhealthy, ethical or unethical, efficient or less efficient and so on.

While we do this in our daily life, we often act on autopilot, barely realizing or questioning too much the conclusions we have drawn; very few of us ever stop to evaluate and actually make a conscious choice of where we want our life to go in the long run. And unless we make a plan, we will end up sliding into other people's plans and wake up ten, twenty years later, frustrated that the whole wide world stole our dreams.

We want to be intentional about our lives. We need a sense of direction and to clearly formulate our desirable outcomes in all areas of our lives: health, spirituality, relationships, career or calling and so on.

How will you reach your destination without know what that is? It is like hopping in your car and driving aimlessly. It's fun for a while (I do it quite often, to relax and think, while listening to my favorite music and audiobooks), but sooner or later you want to know what's the next stop, because you'll run out of gas and into trouble.

You don't want to leave your life direction to "chance", nor to be decided by others, and count on it to turn out the way you want. You cannot expect others to know what makes you fulfilled: that is your permanent and most important job to find out.

So what do we do then? Where do we start?

In order to reach our goals, we need to have a recipe, a strategy, a system for success. A sort of map to our destination, preferably with instructions on how to reach there.

A great approach to life will have you formulating *your goals congruent* or *aligned with your values.* You carry out your dreams and goals through guided inspiration and targeted regular actions (*habits*). And all along you want to cultivate a *growth mindset* and make sure you continue to develop, not stagnate. In other words, you never want to stop growing, allowing your newest potential to evolve and formulate new goals. Contrary to what many religious and spiritual teachings have sold us, we are not here to mortify our senses and lie low, but to constantly flourish into greater wisdom and abundance.

In essence, what congruence means is that your desires are in line with what you think is good, right and achievable for you. To give you an example, if you want a greater amount of money in your life, you will get it as soon as your mind is clear of any doubts, such as: do I deserve it? Is it moral for me to want it, when other people struggle? Can I actually get it? The list is long.

You must have oftentimes wondered "What is it that I really want?"

You may have successfully ignored this question for years, or answered it only partially. We rarely take the time to sit and plan our lives, in the sense of knowing with clarity what we desire.

Yet more and more studies are proving that those who do it are always, always becoming people of great success, because they have abundant clarity on what they stand for, on what motivates them, on the direction and destinations they want to reach in life. And so they have no inner conflicts related to personal worthiness, or doubts about their current or future ability to achieve it.

In the absence of this clarity, we often accept things and situations we do not really want, while we do not go after those that make our heart sing and make us come alive and whole. If only we could consciously wonder, every single day, in every situation, what is it that I really want?

We will face difficult choices, where alternatives look equally painful, or equally attractive. These are the times when your strong values will help clear the way, because you will have a better view of who you are and what you stand for.

Let us make the time now, today for this exploration. This is a powerful exercise that is bound to provide much clarity for the days and years ahead!

One observation: please keep in mind that choosing these values has the purpose to assist you with your main goal: following your joy and loving yourself no matter what. In fact, the values you resonate most with provide extremely precious indicators regarding your joy journey.

You will go through a list of values and select those that most resonate with you, those that feel authentic and true to your heart, the ones that feed your joy and make you come alive.

They may all attract you, and you do not need to exclude anything, but try to focus on those most important for you. The list is not exhaustive, meaning you can add your own values if they are not included already.

It may take you a few days or more to clarify your choices, and that is fine, come back to this repeatedly, print it out so that you can review it again and again. As a result, you may realize that you have been living in accordance with your values; or that you have not been true to your heart, and you want to make some changes and adjustments in your life. If so, do not feel overwhelmed; just pick one change at a time and remember that the idea is to feel good and love yourself in the process.

- o Abundance
- o Acceptance
- o Authenticity
- o Achievement
- o Adventure
- o Authority
- o Autonomy, independence
- o Balance
- o Beauty
- o Boldness
- o Compassion
- o Confidence
- o Challenge
- o Citizenship
- o Clarity at all times
- o Community
- o Competency
- o Contribution
- o Creativity
- o Curiosity
- o Determination
- o Endurance
- o Fairness, justice
- o Faith
- o Fame
- o Family
- o Focus ability
- o Friendships
- o Fun

o   Good looks
o   Happiness
o   Hard working
o   Healthy and fit
o   Helpful
o   Honesty
o   Humor
o   Influence
o   Inner Harmony
o   Joy, good mood
o   Justice
o   Kindness
o   Knowledge
o   Leadership
o   Learning, growth and progress
o   Living life on my own terms
o   Love
o   Loyalty
o   Meaningful Work
o   Meditating, participating in religious and spiritual values
o   Money and financial abundance
o   Openness
o   Opinionated
o   Optimism, positive attitude
o   Organized
o   Peace of mind
o   Pleasure
o   Poise
o   Popularity
o   Recognition
o   Religion
o   Reputation
o   Respect for others
o   Respect for nature

- o Responsibility
- o Security
- o Self-Respect
- o Service, contributing to the wellbeing of others
- o Simplicity
- o Spirituality
- o Stability
- o Success
- o Status
- o Tolerance
- o Trustworthiness
- o Uniqueness
- o Wealth
- o Wisdom
- o OTHERS:

I hope you have enjoyed it and **now to the best part: out of all the values you have explored, choose the top ten fundamental personal values, that are highly important to you and will not be negotiated NO MATTER WHAT.**

My personal top ten non-negotiable values

1.
2.
3.
4.
5.
6.
7.
8.
9.
10.

Chapter 12

VALUES VERSUS NEEDS. KNOWING WHERE YOU WANT TO GO, AND WHERE YOU NEVER WANT TO GO, NO MATTER WHAT

Who are you now? Who have you decided to become? These are powerful questions, and we want to strongly answer them ourselves, not have them defined or validated by others.

We have now actively engaged in the process of determining what makes you tick, what are the core values and ideas that you hold dear, that motivate you.

I strongly encourage you to go through yesterday's exercise, if you haven't already, and really jot down at least ten values, ten identities that are simply non-negotiable for you. This gives you the most wonderful start: before you decide where you want to go, you will know for sure WHERE YOU WILL NEVER GO. And that, my friend, will save you a lot of doubts, fears, procrastination and delays, making your decisions much easier. Before you find out what you want, it is great knowing what you do not want and will never choose, tolerate or accept.

One healthy, sound rule to live by that I have learned over the years is to **not compromise my core values for my needs, and to pay great attention to any conflicting values when making important life choices.**

I would love to share two examples, to illustrate what I mean.

One of my core beliefs about myself is that I am caring, compassionate and kind. This is who I want to be, I admire these values in other people and I do all my best to live my life in congruency with them: to think, speak and behave kindly, to care.

I have been in at least two instances that have severely challenged my ability to stay kind to myself and others.

My son is a very playful, energetic, affectionate and strong-willed character, as all happy children should be. When he was a toddler, I often found myself challenged by his demanding nature and hot temper that would spill over into tantrums on a daily basis. I found my ability to be kind and caring was running dry and I started reacting a lot from a place of frustration and overwhelm. Rather than acting consciously from a place of love and compassion.

It is true that I was going through demanding times myself, and that was not an excuse, but a signal to take the help I needed and make the necessary adjustments to take care of myself and my emotions.

My strong need to "control" the situation and my son's temper became stressing and overwhelming, and for a while I would react very angrily, out of despair and lack of understanding and solutions (stress is just a fear of not knowing how to handle things).

I was angry quite often for a while, and I was changing into this person I didn't like at all, very different from the kind, gentle person I wanted to be.

I knew parenting sometimes takes hard decisions and I thought that sometimes you just need to be harsh to be taken seriously (bing! Limiting belief!), but I just hated the thought of it all. There has to be a better way, I kept telling myself, I cannot see myself doing this for the next twenty years! I am changing into a little monster, and this is just not who I want to be. I knew for sure that I could not live with myself that way for much longer, something had to change. I knew for certain I could no longer tolerate living so far away from my core values.

Long story short, I started learning more intensively about positive parenting and assertive communication. I understood that toddlers most often have a temper because they really have a problem (not because they are spoiled brats!), so it is our job as parents to get better at figuring out what that is, and in taking care of our own needs and not letting our own cup run dry.

In my son's case, I discovered he needed more one on one time with me, he was the youngest one and he never had me for himself, so to speak, and he was in a constant state of insecurity and agitation.

I also started making time and space for myself to take care of my own needs, so that I can regain balance and be the kind of person and mother I truly want to be ("love yourself no matter what" means giving yourself what you need).

In this process, I also found the better way of parenting that I was searching for: being firm when necessary does not mean you cannot be still compassionate and kind. I now acknowledge my kids' demands, problems or feelings with kindness, I offer positive alternatives and choices, yet I remain firm in my decision when needed, while all the time re-affirming my love for them and recognizing their every progress. It works wonders.

Improving on any of our skills is a never-ending process, but now I see the beauty of it all and I am able to enjoy wherever I stand in the present moment. I am more willing and capable of seeing my own progress, and giving myself credit for it. When I fail at sticking with the plan, I get back on track and remind myself about direction, about the kind of parent I resolved to be, without beating up on myself for my mistake. I know that would put me in a very low place, from where nothing constructive will come.

I aim to give myself the same compassion that I give my children.

And that is another great component of "loving yourself no matter what".

Sometimes it takes more life experience and deeper introspection to clarify and recognize some of our values and priorities, and that is perfectly all right, since we ourselves are constantly changing, and have embarked on a never-ending journey of further clarification.

Sometimes we have values that may come into conflict with one another, and such situations may trigger a lot of pain and make for difficult decisions, since both values are important for you. Please keep in mind, *emotional pain is always a sign you are on the wrong track somehow, always a sign to stop, re-evaluate, change your perspective or change direction.*

I didn't know how much I valued freedom and independence until I lost them, until I felt trapped to such a high extent that I was physically suffocating every day. My inner conflict, my confusion and my emotional turmoil were taking over my health and my whole life.

I had always valued love, and loyalty to loved ones, above all else, and this has always reflected in my choices. Yet there was a point in my life where I gave up so much on myself, where I betrayed myself to a terrible extent and accepted situations and circumstances that made me deeply unhappy, because I thought I needed to stay loyal to my loved ones' choices and decisions. I thought I am being loyal to love really.

Such deep compromises are recipes for disaster, as I came to find out. I started to feel trapped, helpless, and hopeless. My self-confidence was below zero, I became introverted, bitter, angry, depressed, overwhelmed, and disappointed with myself and everybody else. I was spiraling down. I couldn't even see a glimpse of the person I used to be, and I didn't believe I could be "normal" again (I didn't even dream of reaching where I am today). I felt the world had given up on me.

In fact, it was I who had given up on myself. It was not my loved ones letting me down and ignoring my pain, it was I. Others only reflect to us what we do to ourselves.

I was the one refusing to stand up for what I wanted and to take what I needed. I was being extremely unkind and cruel to myself and denying myself things I desperately needed, just because I thought maybe this is how life is supposed to be, you just need to lower your expectation and live with it, or this is what "others" expected me to do (bing! Limiting beliefs!). I realized I was growing into a copy of my own beloved mother: her choices, her level of self-esteem, her patterns of reaction. And I knew where this was going, I had grown up watching her choices and the consequences that came with them, and I realized I didn't like this direction at all.

The sacrifices I was making, I would have never expected them from another. If I found my daughter, or a girlfriend making such compromises, I would feel deeply sorry and worried about them. Yet I wasn't really doing much myself, to address my own feelings, my own despair – partly because I perceived myself as a hopeless victim, always waiting for help from others.

These are patterns we learn from others, women especially from our mothers, but this is not a reason to stay there, once we become aware of it.

I had to hit rock bottom and become physically ill before I realized I just couldn't go on like that. Our thoughts and feelings affect our bodies; our actions; our lives.

It took me quite a long time, great emotional struggles with myself, and situations that I had never imagined I would go through, just to figure out how important my respect for myself and my independence were. And to start figuring out who I was, what it was that I really wanted, standing up for myself, learning how to take what I needed without apologizing, feeling guilty, or waiting for approval, and making an action plan of how to reach my goals.

Learning to think, speak and act in an assertive manner, neither passive, nor aggressive, has been one of the most valuable practical skills for life I have ever learned.

When we are passive, we tolerate unwanted circumstances without saying or doing anything, accumulating resentment and frustration inside. Until it boils and spills over into aggressiveness. You want neither. You want to learn how to be assertive. This requires us to understand that we are all equal, we all deserve to have our point of view respected, and we all have the right to reach for what we want. I encourage you to learn more about this.

Circumstances, events and people help us define who we are, and what we want to be about. Sometimes their influence is a gentle, discreet nudge to change direction. But this nudge can grow into a sharp and overwhelming pain, if we fail to attend to the solution.

Always take your emotional compass seriously: when you find yourself unhappy, and in pain, stop and ask yourself what it is that brought that feeling? Is it just an unhappy thought that made you miserable? Is that thought really reflecting reality, or is it an unnecessary repetition of old patterns, an exaggeration maybe? If it is an exaggeration, you know how to work your way into improved perspectives and better emotions.

But if it is a genuine, realistic, legitimate concern, if your reality doesn't make you happy, turn your attention and focus on what you want and make it happen. Stick your thoughts to the desired outcome, and never let go of the improved direction. Stand up for yourself and your happiness at all times.

Chapter 13

HABITS: YOUR POWERFUL ALLIES FOR A CONFIDENT, JOYFUL LIFE

It all starts with a simple, innocent, apparently insignificant step.

Like having that first one cigarette, to impress my high-school friends. That led to the next. Before I knew it, I starting identifying myself as a smoker, and I smoked for over ten years, much more than just one cigarette per day.

There was an equally destructive habit of self-criticism and negative thinking. The permanent inner mean little voice that used to pick on my looks, criticize my words, my actions, mock and shame everything I did really, every single day. The little voice that would remind me of my "defects" and my "failures" day in and day out, putting me in a constant state of shame, discouragement, inferiority, insignificance. The way I talked to myself – God, I would have never, ever talked like that to another human being, yet I was treating myself worse than an enemy. That was just another habit, but how much it influenced the way I felt, spoke and behaved!

Or like giving up my power to others, by choosing to feel like a victim with no options and no support.

We could destroy our bodies, minds and emotions systematically, and many of us do this daily. We could ruin our relationships; blow up our money and freedom regularly.

Or we could be our best supporters, our own personal empowerment coach, our most sympathetic and motivating, caring friend, teacher, mentor, and cheerleader.

It's all a matter of choice, of being willing to face and realize what you are actually doing to yourself, and changing it.

Of learning what to choose that is best for us, others and our highest good, and actually following through in the same direction, relentlessly.

Albert Einstein's words are crystal clear: "insanity is doing the same thing over and over, and expecting different results."

As I committed to give up smoking, I weighed the picture of health, wasted money, smelly smoker identity, ashtray- stinking clothes, unpleasant breath (and its relevance to kisses, yes). On the other side, I saw a healthier body and less wrinkles, a better role model in myself, money saved (that I can use for better things). I decided I would be a non-smoker and never looked back in over ten years. Things to help on the way: do not keep cigarettes at home; drink a lot of water and take deep breaths when I felt cravings; save the money and reward myself at the end of each month; for the first month, do not attend parties/events where people smoked; talk to people who gave up smoking already.

As for the little mean voice, my inner critic that made me miserable day in and day out, I decided I needed to change the dialogues I had with myself drastically. I had two visions before me. One extremely painful: a lifetime of inner struggle, frustration and discouragement, never free of self-doubt and self-hate; never having the courage to go for my dreams; ending up like most of the women I used to see in their fifties and sixties, bitter, depressed, always angry, always frustrated, always reacting, always confused. What a horrible picture, isn't it? What a sad role model I would have offered my kids…!

At the other end, I pictured myself always in charge of how I felt, optimistic, supportive, full of good energy and always ready to give myself and others a lot of love and kindness. The choice was easy.

The secret really lies in painting very convincing pictures for yourself, in your mind. Feeling yourself alive in either of those two movies, the happy scenario versus the horror one. Believe me, you will make your decision in a heartbeat.

We all have habits; the things that we do by default, on autopilot, without thinking much, because they have become familiar and automatized, taken over by our subconscious mind. We link them to some sort of perceived satisfaction, pleasure or reward in our system, often without even realizing.

Some of our habits support and build us up in the most empowering ways, while others tear us down gradually, little thieves carrying us quietly in a totally destructive direction, with small, barely perceptible steps - not for our higher good.

What we want is to choose those habits that will help us create a happy, peaceful mind, love, joy, prosperity, amazing vibrant health and loving, fulfilling relationships.

The way to change? As we become aware of some unbearable consequences of continuing in the same way, we want to focus all our energy on linking the new habit to the tremendous satisfaction of the results we'll get.

We do this with our kids so easily, guiding them towards a pleasant outcome, describing it to them in the most exciting words. We need to learn to do it with ourselves and become our most powerful motivator (or be doomed to remain our own worst enemy).

All successful people have efficient, tested **daily routines** in place that help carry them easily towards balance, progress and achieving their goals. Towards a confident, strong, intentional life, where they fully experience themselves as powerful creators.

Most of these routines will nourish **the four dimensions of our existence and keep your life in balance, great energy and sense of direction.**

Here are some of my own:
- **Physical**
  Examples of routines that will keep your body functioning at full potential:
    - Wake up at 5a.m. to plan your day and have time to pray, meditate, work out;
    - Drink 2 liters of water;
    - Intermittent fasting at times;
    - Meditate 20 minutes
    - Great posture by stretching;
    - Breathing exercises 4-12-8;
    - Workout 30 minutes;
    - Explosive movements and dance on your favorite music;
    - Eating more raw vegetables and fruit daily
    - Switching to healthy fats versus unhealthy ones;

- Give up smoking;
- Practice a sport three times a week, sometimes with a friend or kids;
- Walk in nature; etc.

- **Emotional**

  Examples of habits that support an optimal emotional wellbeing:
  - Daily Gratitude journaling/lists of things we appreciate, in handwriting or using applications such as Happier;
  - Seeing emotions as powerful signals to pay attention to, catch the negative thought, rephrase and take action to change your reality;
  - Using the Emotional Guidance scale;
  - Choosing your feelings intentionally –joy, love, peace, freedom;
  - Laughing a lot;
  - Tell your loved ones how much you love them and hug them;
  - Say thank you and I'm sorry;
  - Have reminders of who I am and who I want to be everywhere: phone, computer, etc.
  - Write gratitude letters to people you appreciate;
  - Smile and tell jokes;
  - Practice EFT and the Emotion Code to release trapped emotions; etc.

- **Mental/intellectual**

  Examples of habits that support best mental well being and intellectual growth:
  - Positive affirmations, with enthusiasm and feeling (with explosive movements, music);
  - Monitoring your thoughts and replace negative, destructive dialogues with empowering, constructive ones;

- Reading every day;
- Learning from mentors and role models;
- Learning new skills regularly, measuring your progress regularly, and aiming for constant improvement;
- Be part of a group with similar interests;
- Hiring a Coach/Mentor to kick-start and guide progress.

- **Spiritual**
  Examples of habits that support best spiritual growth:
  - Prayer and asking for clarity, guidance and inspiration in the morning and throughout the day;
  - Constant desire and willingness to experience the God within, with the senses, with our rational minds and understanding, with our emotion and knowing, until it becomes our daily reality
  - Meditation and cultivating an attitude of appreciation: the ability to find the good and goodness in your life
  - Energy self- healing;
  - Visualizing your day and your desired outcomes for the day;
  - Practicing Ho'oponopono throughout the day;
  - Do one good deed per day;
  - Blessings for yourself and loved ones, etc.
  - Reminding yourself regularly that you are constantly Guided, all you need to do is ask, and opening yourself to receiving the Guidance in any form.

These are examples of the things I do that work wonderfully.

You can play and experiment with any of these – mark them right now- and keep educating yourself on success and happiness habits.

Please remember: enjoy the process, and keep your desired results in mind for you to feel motivated, not overwhelmed. Your constant objective remains to be able to experience the joy along the way, and not to force yourself into any patterns or recipes described by me or anyone else. To like yourself more and more, first a little bit, and then, as you advance in your appreciation, you will one fine day wake up sincerely loving and admiring the person in the mirror. It is my promise to you that this day is coming.

Grow your empowering habits daily, cultivate awareness of Who you are in every moment, and you will soon experience mind-blowing changes and bloom into a happier, stronger and more confident you.

Your time as a caterpillar has expired. Your wings are ready.

Chapter 14

YOUR PEOPLE, ONE OF THE MOST POWERFUL FORCES IN YOUR LIFE

We all live among other people. The relationships we build, and the interactions that we have with others greatly influence our preferences, our values, and our decisions. Our life.

If you decided to be a nun or a monk and live in isolation, you'd most probably talk only to yourself and hopefully the Divinity, or Higher Power, right? (And you couldn't possibly be reading this, because there shouldn't be any Wi-Fi in your hermit cave or monastery!) ☺ Even then, you would still be in contact with people through stories and advice of role models in the books you read, and with memories of people you grew up with.

We are never alone, really.

What is your birthplace like, the place of your childhood?

Is your country at peace, or at war?

Is your family prosperous, or struggling?

Do you come from a fairly balanced family that offered you stability, love and support until your late twenties? Or have you grown up in the midst of the turmoil of some troubled, violent adults? Maybe had to work to support yourself since you were a teen?

Were your friends kind, caring, and focused on growing and developing, or were they negative, even bullying, intimidating and immersed in destructive habits?

I guess you know where this list is going. I'm going to ask you to *consider your friends; your life partner; your work peers; the people you follow in the news and the social media; the books you read and the heroes in the movies you watch.*

Who are the five people in your life that you spend most of your time with? Jim Rohn, one of the most powerful teacher and mentor of all times, concluded that our character, aspirations and daily actions tend to average those of the five people closest to us.

As I look around, and back in time, I know I have always been blessed with good people in my life.

During my school years, I made a considerable number of good friends, too.

I used to come home and, full of excitement, tell my dad all about them. His reaction used to baffle me: more often than not, he would ask me the same series of questions: "Do they study well?", "Who are their parents and what is their occupation?" and so on. A bit awkward, I used to think, even irritating. Why should I care about my friends' grades, and if they study well or not? What do I care about their parents and their background? All that mattered was the way I felt around them, right?

In principle this is true, when our Inner Guidance is turned on, when we are in tune with the God within by cultivating appreciation and joy in our daily life. Very naturally, people will come into our experience to match and mirror what we cultivate inside.

Years ago I spent a lot of time talking to one of my mentors about my relationship with a close family member, a relationship that was draining me of energy and time. One that I had allowed to take a big toll on my emotions, and my ability to live life freely and joyfully.

The advice I got was: give up your expectations, and put a distance if necessary.

I was mad in the beginning. How could I "give up" on a family member? That sounded like abandon, and wouldn't this mean that something was wrong with me, if I was not able to repair this relation, with all my kindness and my good efforts? What about loyalty and unconditional love? How could my mentor expect me to put a distance and give up my expectations?

I stubbornly kept on trying to grow my relationship, wanting to inspire with my love and patience. During this time, I went through many frustrating moments; moments when I had to lower all my standards, face a great deal of negativity and aggressiveness. This had been going on and off throughout my whole life.

When I finally hit the bottom and had nothing left to give, I decided to let go and put a distance between us for a while.

And that was one of the best decisions I have ever made. And it taught me that you don't have to wait until you reach rock bottom emotionally before you cut yourself free from any source of angst. Unconditional love does not mean that you need to lower your love for yourself, or put up with suffering, disrespect or neglect for anybody.

In my country there is a popular saying that goes like: "Tell me whom you're seeing and I'll tell you who you are."

Yes, it is true. We become like the people we spend most of our time with.

I had the opportunity to test this repeatedly, all the way.

For a loved one, I unconsciously changed myself and walked another road than the one I wanted. Let myself slide into others' plans, for I had no clear, strong plan of my own. Only vague ideas about what my life was supposed to grow into.

One day I had an awakening moment: I suddenly realized that I had nearly forgotten all my dreams; I began doubting myself, feeling vulnerable, unworthy, unsafe, unwanted. I found myself suffocating, physically and emotionally and in all ways conceivable. Interestingly, my perceived sacrifice didn't seem to be seen by others, nor earn me any extra credit or recognition with them. The lower I went, the more invisible my efforts were becoming, the more my entire reality was closing in on me, the less people were able to see me in my personal hell.

Sometimes it has to get that bad, for us to have crystal clarity on what we just cannnot, and will not tolerate. Ever again.

And luckily for me, I was pretty strong about my values, and it eventually became evident that I couldn't live too far from them, for anyone else's sake. What I mean by this is that my frustration was growing inside me to giant proportions, and it was taking over like the most poisonous dark octopus of unhappiness and despair.

I was turning into a walking, talking hurricane of anger and sadness, and I hated who I was becoming.

I had almost lost myself.

I realized with intense clarity how vital it was for me to stay loving, positive and strong.

To be able put myself forth in the world in a way that was powerful, kind and full of life.

To be someone I could not only live with, but also love and admire.

I desperately wanted to like, respect and enjoy being me.

Isn't that what we all yearn for, so painfully? The call of our souls, of our higher selves is strong and it never stops, for they see us for what we are, stunning, larger-than-life, amazing Creators!

The ultimate pain that we feel when we are down in the pit is the powerful indicator that we have strayed so far from this core and blessed essence of who we can become.

The happy, confident life we came to live.

It is all part of the journey, though. When you've descended so far in the abyss, the joy you feel when you become yourself is indescribable. It is sheer elation and blissful liberation, day in and day out.

But all these do not mean that you have to skin your knees and shatter your heart at every step, for every single progress, to learn every skill.

You do not have time to make all the mistakes in the world <u>and</u> experience joy and growth.

We can also learn the easy way, and we can then move on to the next level, the next adventure.

If you want to be successful, make sure you surround yourself with the right people: in your physical world, as well as inside your mind - especially those you give importance to, and air time inside your mind, those whose words and actions you keep contemplating on a regular basis.

Our entourage has enormous impact on us, as we get our inspiration and energy from our daily interactions with these people. The way they think, their attitude shapes our lives. You can and should of course, always make sure that you are in the best of moods and tend to your own happiness and growth; but why do it in a place where you are the black sheep, where you face constant opposition, when you could do it among people with the same mindset, people who are happy to have you around, and let yourself be carried forward by the good wave?

We tend to unconsciously try to fit in the same picture, and stay on the same level with our friends, live up (or down) to their expectations, in order to maintain balance and preserve our friendship.

Over time, we borrow their habits (good *and* bad, alas!), their thinking patterns (uplifting *and* limiting). They may stimulate us to grow - the ideal scenario, or indirectly make us lower our standards. Our success may deter and feel threatening to some, as they no longer feel significant and important enough in our presence.

Good friends will pull you up, rejoice in your success, and remind you of who you are during your times of darkness. You don't want the others. Let them go.

What would be possible if the people around you **refused** to let you fail?

What if you had in your life at least one person able to see your full potential – the total sum of what you can become and grow into? And what if this special friend absolutely adored you and was completely on your side, ready, able and willing to guide you every step of the way?

This friend exists. You could call it your soul, your God within, your inner guidance, your higher self. The way to connect with your precious guidance is to simply ask for it persistently and be willing to receive it – when you commit to staying most of the time in an emotional state that feels good to you. To love yourself enough that you will no longer tolerate unhappiness, fear, tension, anger and so on, no matter what.

All roads seem to lead to this same conclusion and solution.

Role models are those guides who shine their lights ahead of you, clearly revealing the path towards your goals.

Their lives, their actions and their values will inspire and motivate you to raise your own expectations and aim much, much higher.

Their examples and their tested strategies will pop up like fireworks in your mind when you face tough decisions, or in times of sorrow and instability.

They will be living guidance, breaking your limiting perceptions and replacing them with a new, empowering perspective. You will have far more fulfilling, greater milestones you set up for yourself and for your life.

Tao Porchon Lynch, the oldest yoga teacher at ninety-seven, a multiple ballroom champion with a twenty-seven year-old dance partner, is an extraordinary example of energy, optimism and love for life. People like Tao and Louise Hay have redefined for me and millions of others what old age can look like, and what it can mean; shattering the frightening debilitating image we were all used to.

They are the vibrant living proof of what you and me can look like fifty, sixty or seventy years from now.

Consider seventy seven-year-old great- grandmother Edith Wilma Connor, who began to feel like the time spent behind her desk was making her stagnant and she decided to take up fitness. She was in her sixties, and what began as simple gym routine with her son turned into a serious pursuit of bodybuilding, leading her to win championships and literally turn her own life and health around.

Bryson William "Verdun" Hayes, the hundred-and-one year young D-day veteran, jumped from a plane in a tandem skydive, with three generations of his family, becoming the world's oldest skydiver. Hundred and one.

Over the years, I have taken the habit of paying close attention to those people who inspire me. I have a list that I keep adding to, with names and qualities I admire.

There is my grandmother with her undying faith in our Creator, her thirst for learning and dedication to family, hard work and honesty, commitment to order and doing things the right way.

My grandfather, the village teacher, who dedicated his entire life to growing others. Loved and cherished by hundreds of people he guided toward better lives.

I see my father's calm, his charm and sincere dedication to helping others; his forgiving nature, sense of humor and his ability to enjoy life fully. His strength and calm confidence that everything can be figured out. His open friendly nature and everlasting loyalty to his friends.

My mother's amazing generosity and dedication to her children, her love for reading and for the beauty of words, the joy she derives from surprising her loved ones with her state-of-the-art cooking; the incredible level of attention that she gives in choosing and offering just the perfect gift to anyone.

My husband's tenacity, his love for God, his extraordinary loving kindness, bright intelligence, multi-passionate character and his wish and willingness to constantly grow and progress.

My brother's gentle respect for all people.

So many friends and colleagues, with an endless rainbow of qualities and inspiring features.

Dalai Lama for enduring love and faith in humanity.

Gandhi and Nelson Mandela, for showing that one man can impact hundreds of millions and create lasting change by his example of non-violent protest.

Jessica Cox, the pilot without arms, who surfs and has a black belt in martial arts.

Anthony Robbins, the giant who lives to serve and empower others.

John Maxwell, creator of extraordinary networks of leaders, cultivating and inspiring values and growth in others.

Blake Mycoskie of the TOMS shoes, whose sheer compassion for barefoot poor kids in South America moved him to build a business that empowers buyers to help these kids across the world.

Countless examples of people who have defeated deadly conditions and defied all odds.

You, for caring for yourself and committing to grow and never give up on yourself, ever again.

While many of our role models are remote characters, not within our immediate reach, it's worth taking your relation with your role model one step further: a mentor would ensure focused specific guidance and give you feedback. Most often she will be physically there in your life, as well. If you know someone you admire, ask them to be your mentor: they will most probably be pleased and honored to help with their wisdom and leadership.

Try to surround yourself with empowering individuals; people you can learn from; people that you look up to.

It may sound difficult to do this, but once you start actively searching, you will notice how often this type of person comes your way, and how open they are to help.

In fact, God's answers to your prayers often come through people.

This has always proved true for me and I have countless real stories to testify. People coming with the solution and help you need, just when you need it. Answers lining up and the next steps lighting up the path before you. I bless them all, every single day, as they have blessed my life beyond imagination.

Now is the best time to take an honest look at the people in your life, and answer a few questions:

Who are your people, those always ready to lift you higher?

Who are those who constantly seem to pull you down?

Who are those people you admire, and for what? Start your list now and keep it open, keep adding to it!

Who would you want to have among your friends? Your mentors?

Chapter 15

FUN TIME – LET'S CREATE YOUR LIFE, THE WAY YOU WANT IT

"The secret to change is to focus all of your energy, not on fighting the old, but on building the new."

-Socrates

Dear friend, you have come a long way already. You must be proud for committing to change your life and to build your confidence by taking action.

You have now gained awareness about your most important, non-negotiable values, so that you know what motivates you, and what you definitely want to stay away from, no matter what.

It is time now for discovering, designing and unleashing the new you, piece by piece.

This powerful exercise is often used by coaching experts and not only, to help you assess your current levels of satisfaction with the main areas of your life.

This is like an X-ray of the present moment. It helps you estimate where you currently stand in terms of health, career, personal development, love and relationships, spirituality and so on.

This is a good place to start, but please keep in mind that **your past and your present do not, in fact, determine your future.**

What determines your future is what you do in the present moment, and how focused you are in your ability to imagine and create a better reality.

So take this X-ray for what it is, just a still picture of your present, a moment in time, and a way of getting clarified on where you need to focus your energy and attention today and in the future.

Ready? Let's go!

SECTOR OF LIFE	Degree of satisfaction (10 is greatly satisfied)
Self Image	
Health/Fitness	
Spiritual	
Family	
Recreation/Fun	
Romance/Love	
Social/Friends	
Personal Growth	
Finance/Wealth	
Career/Studies/Business	
Contribution	

The different sectors identify areas of your life that need to grow, in order for you to feel balanced, healthy, energized and in love with life overall. The chosen areas are generally relevant for everyone, but feel free to add anything else that is very significant in your life.

Obviously, for a fulfilled experience of life, we would want to aim for higher levels in all areas.

When we neglect one or more areas for a while, the wheel will be out of balance, and further areas will be affected. Imagine driving with one or two flat tires on your car: your journey through life will become quite unpleasant, to say the least.

What we now do is go through each life sector and mark how happy we are about it. For example, if I feel that I have been doing a great job on my Personal Growth, I would go for an 8, 9 or 10. If I perceive my relation with my husband as very fulfilling, I will put the same numbers in the Romance/Love sector.

Take your time to think it through and treat yourself kindly in the process (no fear, guilt, shame or panic, we want to feel good, and for that we will focus on appreciating ourselves for the courage to do the work and love ourselves through it). Note down any insights, any ideas that pop up, because they will.

Don't tell yourself you'll do it tomorrow or next week. Do it now, it's worth your fifteen minutes, I promise.

Next we'll get very specific into goal shaping, one of my favorite things.

Getting Specific and Shaping Goals

"I came so that they may have life, and have it abundantly."
-Jesus (John 10:10, The Bible- English Standard Version)

Countless studies have confirmed that **written goals** make a huge difference between success and failure. We all know it, it has become common knowledge, and we often think "we've heard this advice so many times, this is boring and trite". So many things have become common knowledge, yet people still do not act upon them.

What would you do, if you knew you could not fail?

What would you do, if success were guaranteed?

Knowing that whatever we ask for is given, let us examine each sector of our life, and take perhaps the best-spent time to shape and phrase two goals for each area. Two desires for improvement.

There is tremendous power in having your goals written down. It is as if your mind sets in motion all energies around, to conspire and cast out the "fishing net" throughout the universe, and bring in the result of your desire.

If you are not in favor of prayer (and even if you are), writing is the next best thing. It is another way to start your conversation with yourself and your Creator, and give more shape and meaning to your dreams. It is close to meditation, since it allows your subconscious to stream thoughts, solutions and ideas into your conscious mind.

So let's do it, here and now. I have provided some personal examples just to ignite your imagination.

Self Image
(e.g. Learn to love myself, no matter what)

1.

2.

Spiritual

(e.g. Make my awareness of God within my number one priority every day)

1.

2.

Personal Growth

(e.g. Become aware of my life calling; daily read or listen to presentations that improve my understanding of my favorite subjects; learn new skills regularly; cultivate relationships with mentors and role models)

1.

2.

Contribution

(e.g. Ensure to always have a good word of encouragement and appreciation for anyone; mentor people who are younger or less experienced in my field; spread awareness of the importance of nature for physical, mental and emotional wellness)

1. 1.

2. 2.

Recreation/Fun

(e.g. Play every day; practice exciting hobbies like dancing, singing, target-shooting, diving etc)

1.

2.

Romance/Love

(e.g. Make a daily habit of appreciating my partner's qualities and actions, and of reliving together happy memories, as well as doing things we love together regularly; constantly spice up the sense of mutual admiration, authenticity and trust, fun and intimacy)

1.

2.

Family
(e.g. Gift my family members with the happiest, most inspired and inspiring version of me as much as possible at all times; be loving, strong, joyful and supportive and communicate my appreciation abundantly)

1.

2.

Social/Friends
(e.g. Have delicious friendships with inspiring people and build each other stronger; keep in touch with friends regularly and communicate my appreciation)

1.

2.

Health/Fitness
(e.g. Become a CrossFit champion, run a marathon, etc.)

1.

2.

Finance/Wealth
(e.g. Enjoy a disposable income of five hundred thousand dollars a month; own liquid assets of over ten million dollars)

1.

2.

Business/Career/Studies
(e.g. My business provides passive income and my physical presence or involvement is not required for its functioning perfectly; my books have become international best sellers and I speak to thousands of people and help them transform their lives in the most powerful and meaningful ways)

1.

2.

> *"We are what we repeatedly do. Excellence,*
> *then, is not an act, but a habit."*
> -Aristotle

Let's take another giant step closer to your goals, and up the confidence ladder, by mapping the road to your dream.

You will learn a powerful, tested method for translating our dreams from beautiful pictures on a board, into palpable steps, specific actions and empowering habits that will build your way to the goal.

Do remember to be kind and gentle with yourself, and have fun in the process, make it pleasant, learn to use your desire to fuel you into action mode, rather than bring you down and discourage you.

Learning to make changes and implement new habits is a skill and it gets **so much easier** with time and practice, I guarantee.

Have you had the experience of making a decision for change, but then not following through? Maybe you wanted to lose weight, quit smoking, work out daily, take up yoga or meditation, end a toxic relationship, get a new job, open a savings account (and actually saving the money)?

I certainly used to struggle with goals, to the extent that I often used to become so frustrated and give up. Failure after failure would only make my confidence levels plummet and my self-respect vanish. Disappointment in myself flourished and I wasn't saying very nice things to the girl in the mirror.

Some trials and errors later, I learned what you are about to learn. A method that has helped me:

-   Experience life in states of joy, excitement, love, peacefulness, kindness, freedom and awe, most of the time, every single day, for longer than I can now remember. Living alive every day of my life.
-   Modify my inner dialogue from a fearful, pessimistic and self-critical one, to one of empowering thoughts, feelings and attitudes, constructive positive thinking, self appreciation and love, day in and day out
-   Change my career path completely and do what I love and what I am good at, with people who are so grateful to receive my gift
-   Lose the extra weight and work out regularly to keep myself strong and fit
-   Give up sugar for one full year
-   Quit smoking
-   Become a vegetarian (after a one year trial I decided to stay vegetarian and never looked back in the past eight years)
-   Redefine some of the most important relationships with loved ones, for better mutual understanding and loving
-   Make personal development a crucial priority for constant growth And more.

So why do so many people fail to reach their goals?

If you are like me (and the majority of people), it is likely that you used to set up goals with initial enthusiasm and best intentions, but with little clarity about:

1. Your WHAT: a clear target of what you want, otherwise you are wondering in the woods

2. Your WHY: that will bring your desire alive again, hot and strong, in times when you feel far from your destination

3. Your HOW: an initial recipe, system, strategy or plan for action, that you will fine-tune and adjust as you go.

Let's get straight into it and look at them more closely.

I want you to get yourself in top-notch mood, get your happy confident muscles warmed up and your fire going! It is crucial that you are in your best mood. Now pick one of your goals and let's start writing at each step. Come on, this is the time and the place for you to actually experiment it first-hand; once you get the hang of it, you will be able to apply it to any of your other goals! I am "holding your hand" through it and sharing my personal example.

You are in a great mood, open for inspiration. Let's go then.

<u>Step 1 WHAT is my goal?</u>

Define your best outcome in great detail, using an empowering perspective. The more specific, the better.

Bad example: I want to go on a diet
Good example: I want to become fit and strong, able to wear my favorite
    jeans again, able to walk, run, lift my children without straining
    and lose 10 kg in the process, in a pleasant and healthy way.

Your turn now:
My goal is:

Step 2 WHY do I want this?

People do not change unless they really think they have to! You won't actually follow through; you won't make an important move unless you make it unbearable for yourself to stay in the same place, doing the same old things!

At this step you want to write down:

- Why you must change? What will you get if you reach your goal?

Example: I will feel and look healthy, full of energy, strong, fit, and extremely attractive. I will feel top-of-the-world in my body, I will be able to play sports with my kids, jog with my husband, feel comfortable in my body in a nice bikini etc. whatever motivates you goes here:

- What happens if I do not reach my goal?

Example: I have been promising myself for fifteen years that I would do this. If I don't succeed now, I don't think I will ever do it, I tried so many times. I will most likely end up fat, frustrated, disappointed, hating myself and others, missing on opportunities to participate in games, events, and my children's play. I will be a sad unhealthy role model for my children. I will lose my confidence in my ability to carry through with my decisions (this should be enough to freak most people out, this perspective is very hard to face ☺). Write whatever motivates you, in your own words:

- Who will I become in the process? How does my identity change?

Example: I will no longer be the "sloppy-never fit-low-energy- never-happy-with-herself" woman. I will become the fit-strong-good looking-self-respecting-always full of energy best version of me. My body will carry me and help me stay in a good mood, and we will go together to a whole new level. My body is my loyal friend (and the only body I have!), so I commit to give it the best care and become a role model for myself, my family and friends.

Write down how you will see and feel about yourself:

- What limiting beliefs may be in my way to getting there? Write freely here, exploring anything that comes to mind, and give yourself arguments why these beliefs are false, and need replacing.

Example:

- Good-looking people are superficial. – False. There are many kind, amazing good lookers you know. There are also many superficial people who do not look so good.
- My friends will feel threatened by my good looks – You need friends who want to see you excel in all areas of your life, not people who hold you down.
- Losing weight is very tough and it takes a long time – False, it doesn't have to be, if you have the right strategy.
- I don't like working out- Find activities that you enjoy doing, yoga, swimming, dancing, or reduce workouts to short, intensive intervals, watching motivating workout videos (plenty on YouTube), hire a professional trainer to learn most effective strategies.
- I like eating junk food, I cannot give up- go back to the question "What happens if I do not reach my goal" and see if you are willing to face the consequences. Keep junk food to a proportion of 20% only- this way, you won't need to instantly give it all up.

Start writing your limiting beliefs now, my dear friend:

Step 3 HOW do I get there?

To identify the first steps and a possible framework for action:
- Have loads of **fun** in the process, make it an exciting game. **Praise and reward yourself for the progress.** This is very important, because we want our minds to fully acknowledge our new and improved status, the growth and our merit, to further build confidence in our capacity to complete the full journey.
- Make educating yourself about your options the first priority, and learn about the **best habits** that make it easier for you to reach your goal (especially thinking habits).
- Research on **what successful people do in that area, and copy them.** Yes, it is that simple. Stick with people who have already done it, learn from them, adopt their mindset and their energy, and you will soon begin to have results in those areas.
- Identify efficient actions and transform them into habits until you reach your goal.
- Practice daily to stay close to your goal. Identify a daily **minimum** that you are willing and able to commit to, to "stay in the game" and maintain momentum.
- Motivate yourself daily by visualizing what you will get: make a very compelling vision board that instantly triggers strong positive emotions in you, list positive supportive affirmations about your outcome (that you believe in), put reminders on your phone, mirrors, computer, etc. to boost your enthusiasm.

"A black belt is a white belt that never quit."
-Unknown

It is really crucial to find pleasure, pride and empowerment in our constructive habits, otherwise they will not stick. Willpower will only take us to a certain point, but habits that we enjoy, those will keep us going.

Examples of actions/habits:

A.

- **What**: 20 minutes high-intensity interval exercise daily (a combination of weight lifting/ specific exercises for arms, legs, abdomen/ yoga/jogging etc.)
- **With what/Resources**: Keep my dumbbells and yoga mat always in sight; will have specific clothes for this (or not), will pick up a spot in my home where I can always exercise (living room)
- **When**: Daily: 10 minutes in the morning before kids wake up/10 minutes in the afternoon together with my kids/10 minutes in the evening after they sleep.
- **With whom**: no help needed here, but if I wanted to take it to a higher level, I would probably get help from a coach.
- **How to make sure I do it, I follow through**: Commit to a minimum that I am surely willing and able to do, no matter what (10-15 min a day), and work my way up whenever I can. This is more sustainable for me than aiming for one full hour everyday. Enjoy the feeling of my energized, strong, youthful body as often as I remember! Praise myself and my body for our great results.

"Through discipline comes freedom."
-Aristotle

Good habits are just as addictive as bad habits, but much more rewarding!

B. Intermittent fasting and a healthy diet rich in healthy fats, vegetables and fruit. Intermittent fasting is an efficient, healthy tested method that helps shed fat, not muscle tissue, and it improves metabolism and anti-oxidant processes in the body. It is easier for me to implement than any specific diet, because it involves restricting my eating within an 8-10 hours interval (out of 24h), while I can more or less eat what I like (I don't have to worry about very detailed planned meals that usually come with common diets). I stop eating at 6-7 pm for 14 hours. I drink a very hot tea in the evening.

C. Drink warm water first thing in the morning and any time I feel thirsty.

D. Eat when hungry.

E. Keep healthy options always available.

F. See a nutritionist to identify best food options.

G. Speak regularly to friends who have already achieved the success I want.

H. Keep motivating pictures and slogans everywhere, reminding me of my goal.

I. Celebrate the progress, praise and reward myself regularly! Compliment my energy, strong body, good looks, fitting in those old jeans etc.

Now it is your turn: after meditation and tuning into your Inner Guidance, brainstorm in writing all the directions of action you are inspired to take in order to reach your goal.

1. **What (define goal) and by what time deadline:**

2. **What needs to happen (steps) /With what resources:**

3. With whom:

4. How to make sure that I do it, that I follow through:

Congratulations for all your great work and your effort!

Now apply this same process to all your goals, whenever you are ready. The time you spend doing this offers you clarity worth millions.

Chapter 16

LIVE ALIVE THROUGH YOUR LIFE CALLING

You have had a chance to take a nice, clear X-ray image of the current status of your life in its most important areas.

You have assessed your level of satisfaction and now we have started mapping our way out, to create real change, as well as pro-active confidence, to bring you to where you want to be!

We had fun with goal shaping, and explored the magic of constructive habits: powerful, tested routines and practices that myself and so many people of success have understood that we need to include in our daily life, to support progress and momentum during the journey.

Our next step towards solid confidence is finding your life calling, identifying the gift you have within, that gives you the chance to play out your full potential in life. You may have already found it, or you may have an idea; either way, it is worth exploring the following steps for clarity and certainty.

We want to cultivate a sense of joy in even the most ordinary, mundane activities, to experience thoughts of peace or excitement or fulfillment regardless of our current activities. We don't want to wait for special occasions to feel good; we want to use our passion and good feelings to make every day special.

At the same time, there is no doubt that we all came forth with specific talents, gifts or capabilities. And those of us who employ, develop and call upon these talents, those of us who live our calling, experience insane amounts and heights of joy. When we identify our gifts and translate them into activities, we embark on a serious joyride for life.

Step 1. One beautiful tool I strongly encourage you to use is the Jung-Briggs Myers Typology Test at www.humanmetrics.com.

It will provide you with a very accurate assessment of your strengths, preferences and personality features. Besides offering clarity, it also suggests careers and occupations most suitable for your personality type.

Step 2
Further, there are a few very powerful questions for you, to gain great direction and insight into what it is that you can consider your life calling.

I have explored these and several others myself, before I decided to center my calling around teaching, writing and coaching.

I had always found a great deal of excitement, satisfaction and motivation in supporting others to find their greatness within – people who had in so many ways given up on themselves and life.

I had always been a good, empathetic listener and thrived on digging for solutions, no matter what the problem. Seeing people overcome their fears and limiting beliefs literally made me come alive and feel that yes, I have a purpose, and yes, my life has meaning!

These questions helped me connect the dots and see the bigger picture of who I was meant to become. It takes a bit of your time and attention, yet the results are priceless.

Do take the time and answer them, without distraction, even if it takes several days to think and formulate some answers. Go through the questions once quickly, and then get back to the beginning and start writing. Write the answers down in a separate notebook - I promise you that if you don't, you will forget them. Give yourself the freedom to write whatever else comes up, whatever new idea or inspiration presents itself.

1. How do you want to feel when you do your "work"?

2. What websites do you visit often? What kind of books do you read?

3. If you could start a business or career doing anything in the world, what would it be? Write at least thirty options, and yes I am very serious, do it, you will gain much clarity through this process.

4. What would you love to do for others, if you could be paid for it?

5. What skills do you have that could be translated into paid services?

6. What do people often thank you for doing for them?

7.   What tools, applications or online apps do you know how to use better than anyone else?

8.   What do you do in your free time?

9.   What would you do with your life, if money were not an issue?

10. What do people always seem to ask your help with?

11. When do you feel like your best self?

12. What do you value most in other people and yourself?

13. When do you feel most joyful?

14. What inspiration, idea, or vision keeps coming back to you?

15. When do you lose track of all time, because you are so in tune with the task at hand?

16. Who are the people who inspire you with their passion and their purpose?

17. What do you want to be known for?

18. If you could do anything in the world without worrying about time, money or energy restrictions, what would you do?

19. When do you feel the most peace?

20. When are you most happy and free?

21. What do you do most naturally, with effortless ease?

22. What do you currently need in your life very much that you are not getting?

23. What message does your future self have for you? If you could talk to a version of you at 97 years old, what would she/ he tell you? Would she/he feel sorry for any dreams that she/he never followed or explored?

24. When do you feel most alive? What activities, thoughts or things bring you great happiness and satisfaction?

25. Which ones put your heart on fire and make you feel like the world is yours?

As you will go through these questions repeatedly in the next days and weeks, more inspired options will arise and your clarity on your most fulfilling options will be greater. Myself and all my clients and friends who carried through with this process found our answers. No exception. And you will find yours, too, I am sure of it.

Chapter 17

GROWING OR GOING DOWN?

A while back I watched this brilliant documentary, The Mask You Live In, and it moved me to tears.

It explores the roles we push our little boys into from early childhood. "No crying! Are you a man or a sissy?" "Are you a girl, or a man?" Little boys as young as three are bullied into stuffing their emotions and denying them: boys are not supposed to be emotional, that's only for girls, who are weak and irrational – this is the message.

Many of our boys cannot deal with so many negative emotions bottled up – no human can. They grow into depressed, aggressive, suicidal teenagers. Suicidal rates among teenage boys are seven times higher than among teenage girls. They end up drinking or taking drugs to numb their anxiety, and they eventually resort to violence against themselves or others, as an outlet. Ninety-five percent of criminal offenders are men... The conclusion was that we expect our boys to grow into some very unhealthy roles.

The same is true for our little girls, who are bombarded with superficial role models: cartoon princesses whose highest aim in life is to marry a prince; or sex kitten actresses and celebrities, that our daughters will imitate in order to impress their peers and fit in. They grow up thinking their worth is measured by their looks, and they constantly seek validation from admirers.

These are the masks that some of us have pushed our children to grow into. Perhaps not you or me, but enough of us to make it a reality we want to change.

The most important labels are those we accept and own. Those we choose as our identity. We want to be like Connor McGregor, professional boxer, who called himself a champion on public radio, years before he accomplished his dream. Yes, we want to be that clear and determined about our labels, about the way we see ourselves.

What kind of labels have you been giving yourself, and growing into?

What expectations do you have for yourself? For your life? Your partner? Your friends?

One of my favorite illustrations, one that I have kept nearby for years now, shows a cat seeing itself in the mirror as a great, majestic lion.

It speaks millions about self-image and self worth, a reminder for me about who I want to be, and the qualities I value most, the things that fill my heart and life with meaning.

A daily reminder on my mobile telephone reads:" I am positive, strong, loving, happy, abundant, light, inspiring and caring!"

I have screensavers on my phone and my computer reflecting those things most precious in my life: love, God, people, growth, family, kindness, contribution, nature and so on.

My passwords are built around similar concepts too, so I created tens of opportunities for me in a day to be reminded of who I am and where I am going.

The names we assign to ourselves are the labels we grow into. There is no way we can grow higher than that.

If we do not "buy into" ourselves, nobody else will.

There are numerous studies confirming that. You may have a strong desire, but if your self-image, your self-worth and confidence are low, you will never reach your target.

What are the top three qualities that represent you best?

Please stop to think and write three or more qualities, right here, right now. They may be qualities that you have already strongly developed, or they may be strengths that you still wish to develop further.

I am

Self-image is simply about how **you** perceive yourself.

It is a number of self-impressions that have built up over time: What are your hopes and dreams? What do you think and feel about yourself, in body, personality, identity? What have you done throughout your life, who have you become in the process?

These self-images can be very positive, giving a person confidence in their thoughts and actions, or negative, making a person doubtful of their capabilities and ideas. Here we have already spent time together, finding your limiting values and beliefs.

Surprisingly, your self-image can be very different from how the world sees you. Some people who outwardly seem to have it all (intelligence, looks, personal and financial success) may have a bad self-image.

Conversely, others who have had a very difficult life and multiple hardships may also have a very positive self-image.

Your self-image has a very strong impact on your happiness, and your outlook on life can affect those around you. If you project a positive self-image, people will be more likely to see you as a positive, capable person.

See things as they are, but not worse than they are.

See things as they are, and see their full potential of becoming. This is where you have to fixate the power of your imagination and your thoughts, until this becomes your new reality.

See yourself better than you are, to create an exciting, worthy vision of yourself to grow into!

Developing good self-esteem involves practicing a constructive and appreciative attitude towards yourself and the world around you, and knowing your worthiness and value.

Self-esteem isn't self-absorption; it's self-respect and the knowledge that you are valuable, competent, lovable, worthy.

We have already learned that you can build your self-esteem by working from the inside out (by focusing on changing your own way of thinking before changing the circumstances around you. The goal of this positive thinking is to give you a constructive view of yourself, while seeing yourself honestly and accepting yourself, and removing the internal barriers that keep you from doing your best.

We don't want to leave our growth and our life to luck or fortune, or to the plans of another.

We want to consciously plan for continuous growth and improvement – not because we are not enough, but because our purpose here is to joyfully explore our full potential.

Focus on constant growth, continuous improvement, and you will become the powerful captain, steering the boat of your life safely away from the currents, and in the direction of your full potential.

While you grow, remember that love and kindness to yourself and others are the ultimate reality you want to grow into. Not a mask. Your real self.

Chapter 18

IT IS ALL IN YOUR HANDS, REALLY

What a journey, dear friend, it is high time to celebrate your commitment to clarity and joy!

You wanted to learn how to become confident, so that you never feel lost again.

You have come so far and you have gained so much in your understanding of who you are inside and out, and why you are here. Of what builds your everlasting sense of certainty and your ability to tune into and restore your well being again and again, after any confusion, hesitation or fall. You have taken full responsibility for your happiness, and you now know that you create your own reality.

Joy and freedom are your natural right, and no validation, approval or permission is needed from anyone but yourself.

You have powerful knowledge and mighty tools. You have planted the seeds for deep rooted, undying self-trust.

You know that you can become and achieve anything that you desire.

But how do you know if this has been a success – how do you measure your results?

How do you know you have reached your goal of becoming confident?

You feel better than before, more often than before, and it is because of your awareness of Who you are and understanding of how you function.

Because of your constant attention to your thoughts and emotions, which you redirect constructively as often as needed.

You take time daily to appreciate things big and small, things that are going well, aspects of your life you enjoy.

You have a general sense that you are on track and moving forward, you know your values, and you know how to get where you want.

You feel certain that you can become and achieve anything you desire, and you resolved that this is your identity from now on: you are Confidence - profound, grounded, durable Confidence.

My prayer and my deepest wish for you is that you have gently and lovingly grown into your one best friend, who will stand right with you, now and forever. The one who will always love you dearly, and with such strong commitment, that he or she will never abandon or betray you, nor tolerate another toxic idea, presence or habit in your life.

One who knows that feeling any less than confident is no longer the place to be and experience life from: even if contrast is valuable, you know now that suffering (staying in unpleasant contrast) is not necessary, because you can focus elsewhere, or in a different manner.

One who will always know your intrinsic worthiness, believe in your ever increasing abilities, see the proof of your constant progress, tell you the kind words of compassion you need to hear to get going once more, remind you that there is always a way upward, and believe in your high potential and in your unique gifts.

One who will guide you with encouraging and empowering thoughts in times of sadness. But in fact such times will become so rare, because you will no longer tolerate lying low and staying down, since you know that you create your life from your emotional state, that you can experience Joy again and again, that you can live fully on a daily basis.

My hope is that you have bloomed into that person who is awake to his or her power. One who does not require approval or validation in her daily quest for self-love and growth. The person who knows that she needs to accept and support and love herself sincerely before she can love and uplift the world and other people in major ways.

Life is a continuous journey. There is no final destination, because the story never ends: we are eternally unfolding, never ending work in progress, beautiful butterflies learning how to fly, growing stronger and more spectacular as time goes by. The only success that matters (our perception of our own success) is not measured in what we have achieved, but in the kind of people we have become in the process, the way we feel about ourselves on the inside, because that is where we experience life from, the inside.

And so a confident life is first and foremost one that feels good on the inside – in your own terms, not by society, religious or philosophical standards. A life where you are at peace with yourself, in harmony with the world as it is, and happy about your place in it. Comfortable with the present as it is, as you always reach eagerly into an ever better future.

Keep taking steps in the direction of your happy, confident life! Let your accomplishments be more about who you are and who you want to become, about how you want to feel in every moment. Let other accomplishments come second, in terms of importance to you.

Celebrate every little victory on the way, every single time you catch a negative thought and replace it with a constructive one that makes you feel much better. Every limiting belief you eliminate, every new empowering habit that you successfully install! Every time you have become more aware of Who you are and of all the greatness within.

Celebrate the time when you realize you have been flying high for longer than ever before, because it became your habit and it carried you effortlessly!

Conscious miracles happen for those who know Who they are, and stand in this true identity often enough to recognize the magic.

As I look back upon my life, I see an endless necklace of sparkling gems, miracle after miracle, and all my prayers answered. People, solutions, experiences, clarity and love and endless opportunities to grow into a richer, stronger human, with greater abilities to create and experience joy each day.

The latest treasures? The people in my life. Besides family and friends that bless my life beyond description, I meet fantastic teachers, the most splendid and enlightened healers, extraordinarily gifted students, able to make the best of my love and the powerful tools that I share. Beautiful hearts, burning with the desire to grow and contribute together.

Living in one of the most beautiful places on Earth.

Publishing a book about what I love, with the most loving publishing house in the world. We do live in the most magic times of humanity, where everything proves to be possible.

As I pray that my happiness rekindles yours, I also pray that you let your own joy inspire others to hope and reach for more; to experience more bliss, dream more, learn more, become more of whatever they are meant to blossom into.

Stay committed to seeing the goodness in people, and the greatness of what they can become, especially when they themselves can no longer see it.

Dare to think there is much more beyond what society considers it is humanly possible.

Know with certainty that you influence others and our world, that you can become a positive leader and a role model, an intentional force for the good. An ambassador for God.

Yours lovingly,
Alina

The Essence Of Living Alive

A SUMMARY

Understanding your own Divine essence is the basis of it all. This connection will make anything happen for you, when you pray with appreciation and trust, when you stay focused on the positive, on what you like in life, people, things, experiences and of course, yourself.

Love for self and understanding yourself, as a Soul Essence in a physical body with a mind computer and a heart GPS is crucial. It is not only possible, but also very crucial and necessary that you love yourself. It is a skill that you must learn and it is worth all your time and effort. In essence, *loving yourself* means *allowing* yourself to be happy and fulfilled, and *making* yourself happy and fulfilled. It is your work and responsibility to find out how to do that.

You can be happy every day, every hour of every day, and it is you and you alone who can produce this state consistently for yourself. Pain and discomfort occur for more clarity in contrast, but suffering (staying in pain) is absolutely unnecessary, and you always have the choice to choose a better-feeling, empowering perspective. Transforming your emotional state is the one of the most important skills that anyone can learn.

Live life as a prayer. The most ordinary activity is an opportunity to raise your heart with God, in loving and appreciating thoughts. Any activity is an opportunity for devotion through feelings of joy, freedom, love, excitement, and so on.

As you and Divinity are not separated, but a continuum, you and your Inner Being/Soul/God are permanently connected. When you are in tune, you feel pleasant, empowering emotions. When you are not, you feel unpleasant emotions. You are a human violin.

Everything is possible. Anything you ask is given vibrationally as soon as you ask, and is experienced by your Soul/Inner Being. In order to also receive/perceive it in this "material" reality, you must tune your vibration into the emotional receiving range of hope and above: courage, enthusiasm, trust, confidence, love, freedom, clarity, joy, and adoration. The happier the better, for the speed and impact of your realization.

You must learn to gradually feel the certainty and truth of your desire come true - this is faith, and you can train it by directing and re-directing your thoughts to focus on what you want, not on the absence of it. On constantly finding evidence and proving to yourself that what you want is already here, starting to manifest.

You have access to Divine Help permanently. All you need to do is ask. You can develop a language of communication with Divinity, signs that you are ready to receive and interpret, repeating numbers, images, etc

Your desires are very powerful creators that contribute to the world's evolution, too.

You do not need to accept other people's standards for what is humanly possible in any area of your life. You get to decide how strong, healthy, intelligent, prosperous, talented, loved and loving you can be. How long you are going to live. Humanity has broken standard after standard for millennia, and progress is only accelerating.

You can be a" know-it-all". Do not limit yourself thinking that you couldn't possibly know, or find the answers you want – any answers. You have access to unlimited clarity and knowledge at all times.

You can realize the highest levels of spiritual clarity and sustainable, lasting confidence and joy wherever you are (you do not need to be an isolated sage in the forest, you could be anywhere)

Writing goals down in great detail is a very powerful tool to achieve anything you want (a loving partner, a new home, more abundance, etc.) Write down the story, as you want it to be, dream it into existence.

We are constant work in progress, masterpieces unfolding. Therefore self-acceptance and love, constant growth and using our happiness to inspire others are key to living alive.

About The Author

Live fully alive and build a strong character that creates lasting confidence and joy, as well as a successful life – this time on your terms!

I am a Transformational Coach with great passion for building happy, confident people and leaders for a better world.

What makes me feel alive at full potential is helping people treat themselves and the world in a positive and constructive way. Over the years I have turned my gift and passion into my profession.

While I am a Certified John Maxwell Leadership Coach, Trainer and Speaker, and a Certified Emotion Code Practitioner, my skills, my background and my life are diverse.

I come from Romania and grew up in Bucharest and in my grandparents' heavenly village in the green hills of Transylvania. I studied Political Science in Bucharest, International Relations in London and graduated from a Canadian Romanian MBA. I got married on a beautiful South Indian beach and in the Romanian

Carpathian mountains (ahem, yes, to the same wonderful man) and live in Dubai with my husband and our two children.

Before becoming a certified coach, I worked in international affairs with the Romanian Foreign Affairs Ministry and in education for a short while with the Bucharest Academy of Political Science. I honed my business skills in international trade and the healthcare industry.

My skills and passions have always had one converging point: the desire to reach out to people in an empowering way, using all my knowledge and compassion, to help them achieve clarity and enrich their lives in spirituality, finances, career, relationships.

I am an avid reader and my curiosity and thirst for constant improvement have been my best friends. I believe that God, our inner dialogue, education and self-education are our most powerful allies.

I strongly believe love is the greatest healer and nobody needs to suffer - especially not alone.

I used to dream I could reach out and change lives as a politician. I found I was not yet ready for this path, so I decided I would be a force for good in other ways.

Printed in the United States
By Bookmasters